THE SHAPE OF RED

Published in the United States by Cleis Press, P.O. Box 8933, Pittsburgh, Pennsylvania 15221, and P.O. Box 14684, San Francisco, California 94114.

Printed in the United States.
Cover design: Cecilia Brunazzi
Typesetting: Lila Struss/Calgraphics
Chapter head motifs: Barbara Byers/Cecilia Brunazzi

First Edition.
10 9 8 7 6 5 4 3 2 1

Library of Congress Catalog-in-Publication Data

Hubbard, Ruth, 1924-
    The shape of red.

    1. Hubbard, Ruth, 1924-   2. Randall, Margaret, 1936-
3. Biologists—United States—Correspondence.
4. Poets, American—20th Century—Correspondence.
5. Photographers—United States—Correspondence.
6. Feminism. I. Randall, Margaret, 1936-
II. Title.
QH31.H817H83 1988   305.4'2'0922   88-18972
ISBN: 0-939416-19-0 cloth
ISBN: 0-939416-18-2 paper

THE SHAPE OF RED

Insider/Outsider Reflections

Ruth Hubbard and Margaret Randall

Cleis Press
San Francisco • Pittsburgh

To our families, born and chosen

A well-known scientist (some say it was Bertrand Russell) once gave a public lecture on astronomy. He described how the earth orbits about the sun and how the sun, in turn, orbits around the center of a vast collection of stars called our galaxy. At the end of the lecture, a little old lady at the back of the room got up and said: "What you have told us is rubbish. The world is really a flat plate supported on the back of a giant tortoise." The scientist gave a superior smile before replying. "What is the tortoise standing on?" "You're very clever, young man, very clever," said the old lady. "But it's turtles all the way down."

from *A Brief History of Time* by Stephen W. Hawking

And Hah-nu-nah, the Turtle, became the Earth Bearer.

from the Iroquois story of the Creation

Contents

Introduction

We met in Nicaragua. Earlier, on a visit to Cuba, Ruth had tried to find Margaret and was told she had moved to Managua. Then, in 1983, both of us attended the meeting of artists and intellectuals hosted by the Sandinistas; some three hundred and fifty concerned individuals—writers, scientists, teachers, editors, religious, academic and political people—came together in Managua to look at the new revolution and try to understand what was happening there, what it meant. Late one afternoon Margaret said to Ruth: "Instead of going with the others on the bus, why don't you come with me in my car? We'd have a chance to talk . . . "

We haven't stopped talking. In one of her letters, Ruth remembers the immediate identification, how we both recognized the need to connect. Over the next four years our friendship has grown: in letters, phone calls, visits. In Boston for a reading or lecture, Margaret stayed with Ruth in Cambridge. Once, after a conference in Utah, Ruth stopped over and visited Margaret in her southwestern mountains. When the U.S. Immigration and Naturalization Service (INS) began deportation proceedings against Margaret,

Ruth got together with a group of people in the Boston area and started a defense committee.

Sometime in 1986 we began to use the term insider/outsider. We saw that we are defined as insider or outsider by our country as a whole, by the cultural milieu in which we move, by our mentors and peers, by family (the one in which we grow up and the one we engender, if we do), and by colleagues and co-workers. The ways in which all of these people and groups of people see us affect how we define ourselves. And every possible combination of all these ways of seeing, defines the way we are.

We were not trying to provide some new category or facile blueprint, one more in the seemingly endless collection of structures upon which to hang yet another theory. Rather, insider/outsider has come to be our shorthand way of expressing a feeling, a sense of ourselves in relation to the often ill-fitting or unacceptable definitions placed upon us by a distorting society. A way to talk about questions that don't necessarily—or completely—find a space for themselves within the academic constructs or political formulations to which we might otherwise subscribe. We have been less interested in conclusions than in the search, as excited by process as by the product.

These letters are about identity. Who are we? The unaging white middle-class properly cleaned and pressed dependent and subservient slightly dissatisfied but striving females whose lives are mostly over. Or rebellious questioning angry joyous anguished strong women resisting the media hype offered as mirror, proud of the gray in our hair and vividly concerned with changing the world? When are we one, when the other, when some uncharted combination of both?

As we continued to share ideas, we agreed that insider and outsider are not mutually exclusive. We are usually both at the same time and in the same place. Nor is it always more desirable to be one than the other. There are situations and times when being outside is far preferable, when being inside would be debilitating, confining, corrupting. And there are others, we knew, when what we most want is to be inside, when being outside is exile. As we talked, we began to recognize that it is the tension, the dynamic and dialectic, that matter. Not only matter, but energize us.

Once we agreed that we were interested in exploring insider/
outsider issues—in our particular lives and in the world we
inhabit—the National Women's Studies Association's Tenth
Anniversary meeting in Atlanta (summer 1987) provided a first
arena in which to test our ideas. We submitted a proposal to hold an
informal discussion on the theme at NWSA. It was accepted, and we
were pleased at the excited response from those who participated
with us. We taped that session. There was talk of publishing a
version of the tape.* Listening to it, what became immediately
apparent, though, was that we had barely scratched the surface.
Rather than put that superficial beginning into print, we decided to
keep on talking . . . and writing. Which meant, given our physical
locations, a series of letters we were by that time taking quite
seriously.

We talked about how our feminism informs this journey. One
of us a scientist, the other an artist, we agreed that the *ways* in which
women have dared to share ideas and observations—free of the
competition which characterizes so much of male-dominated
thought—encourages this kind of open-ended exchange. The letters
racing back and forth from Woods Hole to Albuquerque, from
Albuquerque to Woods Hole, not only became provocative and
important in our lives; we wanted to share them. When Margaret
moved east for a year to teach in Hartford, the work became easier.
Ruth's wonderful retreat on Cape Cod made some of the sessions
especially enjoyable.

As women, political beings, and feminists, we naturally looked
to our own experience. We wrote about our origins, childhoods, our
growing up years. We shared observations about broad areas that
define us: belief systems, work, womanhood, sexuality, mothering,
political ideas and activism. References to past and present
dialogues, issues which divide or unite, some of the concerns of our
times, naturally find their way into this conversation. We haven't
tried to avoid them. Neither would we pretend to have exhausted
them.

Our conversation, which is this book, is built around examples,
events, moments in our lives and the lives of others that illustrate

*We thank Shane Snowden and E.J. Graff of *Sojourner* for transcripts of the tapes.

how we have felt insider, outsider, or both. Our accounts are not analytical structures or definitions of "truth," "that's how it is." We suggest openings, ways to organize experiences and think about them, ways to acknowledge and value them, whether they have felt good or bad, important or insignificant. We agree about most things. Where we don't, we have not tried to force a unified vision. This is much more a rememory,* an impression. And that's what we want it to be.

Since we have found it useful and energizing to think about our lives in this way, we hope that you will be stimulated by reading our letters to venture on useful journeys of your own. This kind of unfinished exploration allows for attention to nuances and shadings often lost in sweeping political analysis or careful scholarly work. *What you have here is not the shade of red, but the sound of red . . . the shape of red.*

October, 1987

---

* We want to thank Toni Morrison for inventing this wonderful word. From *Beloved* by Toni Morrison. New York: Alfred Knopf, 1987.

Letter One

What is Inside and what is Out?

Albuquerque, New Mexico
July 26th, 1987

Dearest Ruth:

It somehow seems fitting to begin this letter—or series of letters—on July 26th.* Doing so reminds me of a poem I once wrote, called "Catching Up With Moncada."

It must have been the end of 1972, and I was living in Cuba. Some of us, foreigners (outsiders?), were asked if we wanted to write something for the twentieth anniversary of the attack on Moncada Barracks, the first action on the Cubans' long road to freedom. I guess most people who came up with anything at all produced essays or short pieces: "What the Cuban Revolution means to me," or "What the Cuban Revolution means for Latin America."

I tried the essay route, then found myself writing in verse. The poem begins: "In 1953 I was in high school / in Albuquerque, New Mexico—the young provincial / American middle-class girl. / My

---

* July 26th is the Cuban national holiday, like July 4th in the United States. On that day, in 1953, a small group of revolutionaries, led by Fidel Castro, attacked Moncada, the second largest military barracks in Latin America. The action was a military failure, but sparked the struggle which, by the end of 1959, liberated Cuba from the Batista dictatorship.

hero was still the captain of the school football team. / The word REVOLUTION was never mentioned at home / or anywhere else . . . "

Several *leitmotifs* run through this poem. One of them has to do with the North American sense of conquest. The first stanza, for example, ends with these lines: "Moncada wasn't mentioned / in the ALBUQUERQUE TRIBUNE or the ALBUQUERQUE JOURNAL / or if it was I didn't read the news, / as distant to my life as the recent Korean War / I still thought 'we' had won." Later on there are the lines: " . . . somewhere along the way / I did learn that 'we' hadn't won the Korean War / but we hadn't lost it either," and finally: "by (that) time I knew the Korean War had been won by Koreans . . . "

As useful as it then was for me to understand that the Koreans are an autonomous people with their own interests, much later, of course, I would see farther—to the fact that *no one* was really the victor in that war; that the United States set the Korean people up for what would turn out to be years of suffering and a divided country.

Nevertheless, today I find the references in that poem as useful as any for beginning to examine the insider/outsider nature of my life. They grew out of assumptions produced by disinformation. And the lines of verse follow my own process of demystification as I "unlearned" what media and school texts were diligently teaching me—and millions of others. In a society in which authority (in whatever form) disinforms, trivializes, tantalizes, fabricates needs, and teaches us to mimic rather than to reason, we find ourselves becoming more and more outsider to our real needs as we strive to move more and more inside.

Marshall McLuhan's idea that "the medium is the message" is more of a reality all the time. The vast newspaper-reading (and today television-saturated) American public is conditioned to see the world and its personal place in that world in a particular way. It is always the way that most sustains and nurtures capitalism. Therefore, this way of seeing is by its nature classist, racist, sexist, heterosexist, ageist, able-bodyist and all the rest.

Insider to the American Way of Life of those years—my growing up years—included the notion that any war we fought was a good war, and (as continues to be true for white male thinking in general): we always win.

On my particular journey I fit less easily the model of "insider" when I began to have doubts about who won in Korea. When I finally understood that there are such a people as the North Koreans, with their own identity, history, politics, culture, and needs, I could readily understand that they had won their war. We had lost it. In the process I became at one and the same time more of an outsider vis-à-vis the mainstream beliefs and values of my country and more of an insider, if by that term one means someone closer to the core of her own authentic identity.

Do you remember, Ruth, that when we first began to talk about the idea of insider/outsider, one of the first things that seemed apparent to us was the need to pose the question: *what is inside and what is out?* Whom do we allow to define the terms for us? How do we examine each and every assumption, not only in order to arrive at the most rudimentary analysis, but even to construct a common language with which to speak?

We are constantly made aware, sometimes painfully, of the degree to which insider/outsider concepts operate in our lives. And when we talk about demystifying those concepts, one demystification leads to another; it's almost like that Dutch Cleanser image which has become such a metaphor in much of what I think and write: there is always one more little figure of a prototypic Dutch girl holding one more can of Dutch Cleanser which in turn has one more picture of the Dutch girl holding yet another tiny can of cleanser, and on and on.

In our contemporary media-oriented culture, in which television controls our sense of inner self, as well as our sense of what we should look like, how we should move and speak, what products we need and how to acquire them, what jobs we must aspire to, whether, with whom, and in what ways we must couple, how many children we should procreate and what we must expect of those children—in this media-oriented culture the insider/outsider lines are very specifically drawn.

One class (the class in power), one race (white), one gender (male), and one sexual orientation (hetero) sets the standards for what is in and out. In a country where the myths of freedom (free enterprise, freedom of religion and political persuasion, freedom of expression) cover tremendously subtle and powerful mechanisms of control, our very ability to think and reason is replaced by the pressure to be patriotic, successful, conformist, anorexic, nice. These attributes, in the definitions established by those in power, constitute what is generally accepted as inside.

One of the things I don't want to do much of, at least not at this initial point in our discussion, is theorize. I want to begin by exploring how societally-defined attitudes and my own attitudes about the insider/outsider syndrome—the second increasingly separate from the first—have developed and changed, and how those changes have changed me.

For this I'll need to say some basic things about my origins. But I think I'll save them for my next letter. Waiting for yours, I send all my love,

Margaret

Letter Two

Woods Hole, Massachusetts
July 26th, 1987 (hadn't noticed the date till just now!)

Dear Margaret:

When we first started thinking about insider/outsider, it seemed such a clear distinction: "inside" is the white, male power structure, "outside" are the excluded—women, people of color and especially women of color, poor people, immigrants—all those who are not part of the power structure. But now that I've begun to think about how the insider/outsider axis affects my life, I realize that the situation is a lot more complicated and ambiguous. I see a tension between being inside and outside at the same time and at all times, and not just in different situations but in the same situation.

Take being a woman, outsider to the male power structure. But in a sense, so are most men. That's what is so alienating about power hierarchies, that they ride on creating a mythic "inside" that makes everyone, except the few individuals who manipulate it, feel outside. And as a woman and someone engaged in the struggle for equality across many dimensions, I am not just excluded from that inside, but *want* to be outside it. At the same time, the moment I sense the collectivity of comrades, friends, family, the places where I am not on guard, that becomes the real inside, the inside that matters. And that's one of the things I've begun to realize, that even when we are most outside, we invent, resurrect, construct a history and reality in which we can feel we are insiders. Jews have done that, women have done it, Black people have done it. And it doesn't matter that much whether our history is invented or real (though it's important to distinguish between the two). What we want it for is a space in which we can feel inside.

But I also get a lot of strength from feeling that I am outside, from *refusing* to identify with the power structure and therefore refusing responsibility for how it behaves. I disidentify a lot, at work and in politics. And that, too, is double-edged.

For example, about fifteen years ago when I first joined the biology faculty at Harvard, I was one of five women in my department. I was the only one with tenure, but we all participated in running the department. Now all the others have gone elsewhere (one by choice, the others because they didn't get tenure) and there is only one, new, untenured woman besides myself. The difference is that when I first came two of the more influential and, of course, tenured men, both not accidentally married to women on the faculty, had begun to bring women into the department. Since then, both have left. So, now there is me sounding like a broken record, while the other, male, faculty talk piously about wanting the best person for the job and then define the job and "best" in such a way that every new appointee is a man. (As you know, nothing is easier.)

But by declaring myself an outsider to my department, in terms of my scholarly and political interests and the hierarchical ways my colleagues teach their courses and administer the department, I have jeopardized my effectiveness in departmental politics and virtually eliminated myself from the decision-making process.

I justify this by saying that I can fight only so many battles and that Harvard is not the arena that is most worth tackling; that being one of the oldest, most tradition-bound universities, it will never be in the forefront of progressive change; that it will remain a bastion of conservatism, and will change only when the rest of society changes so much that there is no alternative. I also tell myself that to the extent that I do spend time working for change at Harvard, I can use my energies more effectively by working with students than with my colleagues, whose interests lie in preventing progressive changes, not in making them happen. But what it boils down to is that I like to work where I feel supported and comfortable and I

Ruth in Woods Hole, 1983

don't feel that way at Harvard. Also, by declaring myself an outsider, I get myself off hooks I don't want to be on.

My personal history, and I will tell you lots more about that in a later letter, has made me feel comfortable in outsiderland, constructing cozy inside enclaves within it. I have been trying to think whether I feel weakened or disadvantaged by being an outsider in one of my various axes of insider/outsider tension, but cannot come up with any. It may mean that I so reject the stance of victim, and need to feel in control of my fate, that I am not letting myself feel or see it. Be that as it may, if I survey my various outsiderdoms, whether forced or voluntary, I don't regret any of them or perceive them as detrimental. On the contrary, I feel privileged to have arrived at a position where I don't have to integrate myself into work or political situations—become at least a quasi-insider—in order to survive.

But what does it mean to be an insider or outsider in the larger culture? Every culture defines what is appropriate and necessary to be an insider. This is true of tribal cultures, of the so-called developing ones, and of industrialized ones. Socialist, communist, capitalist. That's what it means to be a cohesive society. What's different about the United States is that here the situation is mystified by the pretense that we have freedom to choose to be anything and anyone we want. In frankly traditional cultures, everyone knows what's expected and that they must fit in. (Some traditional cultures are more tolerant than others about what happens if you don't, and provide niches for people who are "different," like the *berdache* among some American Indians, who have permission to cross-dress and otherwise behave like members of the other sex.)

At the heart of the mystification of insider/outsider in the United States is the idea of the melting pot which says "everyone can be an insider," the operative words being "can be." In a culture with clearer lines—where once an outsider, always an outsider—people don't break their asses to get in. Here in the United States the myth of infinite adaptability and malleability means that people try their damndest to get inside, and no one acknowledges that that means they must deny being who they are and must fit the

22

patriotic, successful, conformist norm. I think that's part of where the craze about Ollie North comes from (though he, too, now has had his twenty-four hours in the limelight). He incarnates the insider stereotype—male, handsome, brave, loyal, dutiful—that we are all supposed to melt down to. The melting pot is perfect for making everyone feel they are outsiders because we are all supposed to melt to the appropriate size and shape, and most of us cannot.

When my family and I were in Cuba in 1981, our hosts took us to the Isle of Youth to visit some of the schools for foreign youngsters. We immediately began to ask each other why the children from different nations were "segregated" into their own schools and not "integrated" into international schools. Why were the Cubans passing up this opportunity for forging international solidarity? It took us a while to realize that we were trapped into the melting pot ideology. The Cubans' whole point was to help these children preserve their cultural and national identification. Then they could join people from other cultures with a sense of their own national identity and history and language. This would protect them from being floundering outsiders in some hypothetical insiderland where they would be prey to the racist, sexist, heterosexist brand of "integration" that is supposed to melt us in the United States into the norm that those who have power define for us and that makes us outsiders to ourselves.

I'm beginning to wonder what the terms insider and outsider really mean. I notice that I often use them in a very personal way. That what I usually mean by being an insider is feeling connected, open, porous to my surroundings—people and places. And what I mean by outsider is erecting a wall around myself, enameling my skin, so that people and places don't make contact with me.

When I say I am an outsider at Harvard, what I mean is that I don't connect with anyone in my building or my department; in a sense, I shut them out as much as, or in some instances more than, they shut me out. Of course, there are also situations where I feel shut out, where it's not my initiative, but my response tends to be the same: the enamel, the wall around myself, so that it doesn't feel very different.

Similarly what I mean by insider is what has happened between you and me. Though we barely knew each other, both of us took the risk of opening up, becoming porous, more porous than I usually do with people I know as little as we knew each other. We had barely met in Managua when you asked whether you could send me your journal. I failed to reach you to say goodbye before returning to the States, so picked up the phone and called you from Woods Hole because I didn't want the connection to be broken. Although we had probably talked no more than four hours, if that, we were—or wanted to be—insiders to each other. Does this jibe with what you mean?

At a less personal level, out in the world, what intrigues me is that when we first began to think about this, I expected the boundaries to be much sharper. Instead, they seem fluid and permeable. And just as there are advantages to being an outsider, there are disadvantages to be an insider. Being inside can be confining, too public, with too little space for privacy, like living in a small village where everyone knows and watches you and comments on everything you do. Or like being a member of a rigid church or political association. Being totally outside is no good either and shades over into being an outcast, someone who is excommunicated and cannot do anything about it, like a Jew in Nazi Germany or a Black person in South Africa. (Your situation vis-à-vis the Immigration and Naturalization Service is different: they would accept you as an insider if you were willing to deny your political opinions—like the people who named names when they were called before the investigating committees during the McCarthy days. If you did that, you might become an insider to them, but you'd be an outsider to yourself and your comrades, family, and friends.)

Even in my closest relationships, there is the inside/outside tension and sometimes the sense of invasion when the other person wants too much, or to get into my thoughts or feelings too deeply, perhaps not what would be too deep at all times, but is right then. The need for privacy, separation, which I have been told I have to a rather exaggerated extent, means that I need to keep others—even very close others—outside and only let them in when I want and on my terms.

24

I suppose that is part of what is so devastating about incest or rape, the lack of respect for boundary, the forced entry of someone who not only should be outside, but should respect my saying—not begging or imploring, merely saying—that they aren't welcome to come in any further.

That is what respect for children means, to acknowledge their boundaries and stay outside without having to be kicked out. To be sensitive enough to know when it's time to get out or where there's a place to stay outside of all the time. A lot of our hidden, or not so hidden, injuries grow out of people blurring those limits and boundaries.

People say that prisoners who have been tortured irrevocably lose a part of themselves. Surely that must be true, but I also hope and gather from what I have read that being able to keep clear both the outsider relationship to the torturer and the inside relationship to yourself and your comrades is what enables people to resist and, when possible, survive and heal.

Clearly, one can gain strength from being an outsider and feel debilitated by staying inside, feeling one must compromise, do things one isn't sure one should be doing, in order to stay inside. (In a sense, become an outsider to oneself.) This makes me wonder what it's been like for you to be an insider in places like Nicaragua and Cuba, where you are in sympathy, and generally agree, with the official inside. Is it all positive or does it have a flip side? My inside situations have always been off the mainstream, so I have no idea what it's like to feel part of the official inside. Another question I have is: are there situations that are so confining and no-exit that there is no escape, and one cannot move outside? I suppose childhood physical and sexual abuse are such situations. Yet also there, in their accounts and memoirs of such invasions, people speak of walling themselves off—even as children. Escaping into themselves or to someone they trust, when they cannot get away from the abusive situation. Of course, those who tell us this are the survivors, the people who have been able to move outside sufficiently to be able to speak or write about it. There must be those who don't succeed, who would like to become outsiders, but are trapped inside.

On a more optimistic note, I am glad the insider/outsider relationship is coming to look so fluid and dynamic. I must confess I was worried that we might be setting up yet another dichotomy. That's what the boys have been up to for a long time and I would hate for us to construct another in that long line of dichotomies, like good/evil, damned/saved, madonna/whore, male/female, or even the milder, more mutually inclusive ones like yin/yang or anima/animus. It's all too easy to put on yes/no spectacles and then see the whole world that way. To me the crux is the dialectic, fluidity, and interpenetration of insider and outsider.

I have thought of a symbol for us. It's a Möbius strip: a strip of paper with a half-twist and the two ends glued together—in other words, a closed, circular strip with a half-twist in it. If you travel along it, starting at any point, say on the outside, you are shortly inside, then outside again, then inside, on and on as you go round and round. There is no demarcation or point of transition between inside and outside. Do you like this image as a way to convey the ambiguities and continuities of insider/outsiderness? Write soon!

Much love,

Ruth

Dignity has Bone, Muscle

Letter Three

Albuquerque, New Mexico
July 30th, 1987

Dearest Ruth:

Interesting that we both chose to initiate this correspondence on July 26th! At the very least, we were in some sort of splendid communication with one another.

In my last letter I said I would have to go back and look at my origins to establish a basis from which to speak about insider/outsider issues. That's what I'll do now.

I was born in 1936 into a white middle-class family in New York City.

The above paragraph didn't end there, but in the middle of writing it, I got into a discussion about class with my brother. I have always thought of my family as middle class. But what does that mean? My brother argues that both my parents' families, my father's more than my mother's, eventually lived primarily from the shares they held in corporate America. Both grandfathers worked all their lives, but by the time my parents were born their livings depended more on their interests in the stock market than on their salaries.

My father, in turn, worked all his life. He worked hard. But, again, our lifestyle was more dependent on inherited wealth than on the fruit of his daily labor. I said that as we did not depend on the sale of my father's labor power we cannot be said to have been working class. Clearly, we were not ruling class: we did not own the labor

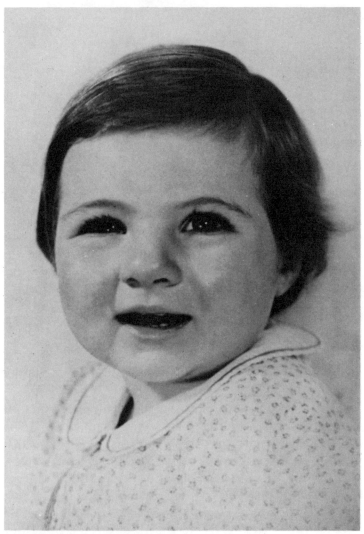

Margaret, age two, New York City, 1938

power of others nor—more importantly—were we in any way connected to the policy-making structure. And so, I thought we were middle class.

But my brother said no, we were upper class. My brother doesn't use the term middle class.

Be that as it may, like much of this transitional generation we had bits and pieces of various ideologies—to go with whatever class we might be. On the one hand, my father worked hard as a school-teacher, we were taught to save in every conceivable way, and even I, the oldest, often wore hand-me-down clothes. On the other hand, we always had a nice home—which my parents owned—a car, and exciting family trips in the summers.

There was a definite work ethic taught as we grew up; learning to support ourselves was seen as important. My parents were and are extremely generous with their children. There are no strings attached to this generosity. There is an ongoing contradiction, though, at least in my mind, between the accounts they keep of small monies owed or owing, and the surprise of immense gifts which provide the givers with as much pleasure as they do those on the receiving end. Perhaps this contradiction reflects their own discomfort around the meaning of money in our lives.

My father comes from a self-made and eventually well-to-do German Jewish immigrant father and a first-generation mother of German Jewish descent. He was the youngest of three sons, and increasingly uncomfortable with the business image his father projected for them all. Although he graduated from the University of Pennsylvania's Wharton School of Business, and tried different business ventures for a while, he finally realized he had to break with his family's values and lifestyle; he drew closer to his love of music (he plays the cello) and moved to New Mexico where he became a public school music teacher, a job that gave him great satisfaction until he retired.

My mother comes from a mixture of German and Scottish non-religious Jewish stock. Her father was a traveling jewelry sales-man who later became a Christian Science practitioner. He was also an adventurous and sometimes unpredictable person, whose fortune rose and fell according to ventures that seem sometimes to have been well-pondered, sometimes pretty crazy. She was the oldest child—with one younger brother—and she was early given to artistic inclinations. After some middle-level schooling she went for several years to the Art Students League, where she began to sculpt. Much later, when I was a teenager, she went to college, making her way through all the available Spanish language and literature courses, some of them more than once. She became a fine Spanish-English translator.

My father's and mother's marriage was in itself something of an outsiders' act for the times, especially from my father's family's point of view. My mother's family, as I said, was not religious. In other ways as well she probably failed to fulfill the daughter-in-law image his parents envisioned. Together, my parents instinctively sought a way out of the socially prescribed and stultified existence that characterized the early years of their marriage and my own childhood.

As the oldest of three children, even though female, I was closer to the insider category than to the outsider. I often found myself acting as a bridge between the adults and my younger siblings. This bridge role would continue to be important later in my life.

Just the other day, I wrote a poem that expresses some of the insider/outsider feelings I had as a young child:

Under the Stairs

My childhood place beneath the family's stairs
was home to Mr. Beeuff, Miss Level, Camp, Girlie—
faithful friends who came
when there was no one else.
Instantly available, invisible to eyes

unprimed to take them in
or on.
We talked endlessly then
through years when Radio let imagination live
and presidents still died natural deaths.

Mr. Beeuff and Miss Level were adults. Ageless
in maturity and sedentary power.
His lined face and lunch pail.
She a nurse in crisp white service.
Years, then, of righteous wars, defense plants
and defense of honor.
Her hands were always clean.

Camp wore a leather jacket, rode a motorcycle,
was my male hero. Power and comfort
in the same breath.
Girlie was just that, *his* girl,
pliant, pretty in whatever image of pretty
lit my eight-year-old eyes.
"No ideas but in things," Williams would say,
but what of ourselves as things? What about service?

When asked about Pearl Harbor
my friends told me wars were o.k.
Not to worry, as the saying goes. Today,
my own wars vying for room inside my chest,
I trace murky reason to those ready answers.
My body is just now my own. My pain
sits towards the back of the theatre. Chewing its nails.

Roque rides a bus, heavy volume of Che
on his jostling lap. He laughs.

How often now has the thousand dollars for Alvaro
changed hands?
Alvaro, José Benito,
interchangeable names in the single focus of death.

Liz says it's true, years ago she was shy
and had to work hard to bridge the deficit.
Debts never canceled somehow, debtors
still looking for a place to stand up,
a place to say: I am.
When the body goes, can we say our work is done?

Mr. Beeuff might be a P-Niner now, his lunch pail
tired of the old liverwurst sandwiches,
pickles and chips.
Miss Level will not deal well
with images of raging skin, pieces of bodies
cracking her memory
after Korea. After Vietnam. El Salvador.
Camp chooses himself. Girlie remains size eight.

Carlos' blue eyes pierce my poem,
Violeta's wound opens again and again
in my own right temple.
Light fades on Havana's seawall, brightens
over my mountains, whimpers in my hands.
We are always going home, going home
wherever memory stands up, says it's time.
Right now. It's time.

On days like these I take the silence
and the sweetness of these men and women
crowding my memory
waking through the cold of that
which is empty, unfinished.
I grab their breath, their teeth,
and tell them what I've learned:

It's not true
a child has no memory before the age of two.
You cannot solve the problems of the planet
in the space for lovers
but lovers can live in the world
if they work at it.

Dignity has bone, muscle.
There is no such thing as absolute truth.

We talk a while, under the stairs.
I talk and listen as I did then.
They come and go, as then.

Well, it's a poem about my childhood and also, of course, about my adult memory of all that. I think the references to my imaginary friends speak particularly to insider/outsider questions.

Getting back to my narrative: as a mother, I now see both oldest and youngest children as insiders. The oldest always has certain privileges bestowed by age; the youngest is the "baby." The middle child becomes the outsider. In our family I think this was true of my sister; at least that is the role she assumed because of the rest of my family's values. In society at large she undoubtedly would be considered the insider. This situation repeated itself years later, with my own children—except that the intensity was diminished somewhat by the fact that I had four, where I had been one of three.

Until I was ten, my parents and my younger sister and brother and I lived in a series of suburban towns within commuting distance of New York City. Then in 1947 my parents decided they were thoroughly tired of the values and expectations built into the life they inherited from their families. They loaded all of us into a black Studebaker sedan and toured the country, looking for a new place to live. After a summer of travel, they stopped in Santa Fe, New Mexico and fell in love with its multicultural beauty. Then they settled on the larger city of Albuquerque, believing its size would afford better job opportunities for my father and better schools for us.

I think our arrival in Albuquerque coincided with my first conscious awareness of being inside or out. Conscious, I say, because looking back on my life I realize that coming to my identity was always problematic—from my infancy (which included sexual abuse from my grandfather), through my child-hood choice of four imaginary friends over a variety of flesh and blood ones, up to and including my teenage decision to be a writer, and thus somehow different from the milieu's socially accepted norm. But in Albuquerque in 1947 I can remember walking across a particular downtown street, looking at the people sharing that space with me, and consciously asking myself: will I ever get to know these people? Will they be my friends?

Being transplanted, so to speak, in the middle of fifth grade, wasn't easy. I longed for a group, girls and boys my own age. My mother accompanied me to several different Sunday church services; my family had not been particularly religious although I had earlier attended, at different times, both Christian Science and Quaker Sunday schools. With the move to Albuquerque I explored other denominations, and settled on an Episcopal church in our new neighborhood, attracted I think most of all by the lure of ritual and what seemed like an inviting group of young people.

This brings me to what I now see as having been a constant in my life: the tendency to throw myself totally into that with which I choose to engage. There was never anything timid or half-way about my commitments. At the age of eleven I became a zealous convert, getting baptized, being confirmed, even—as I remember it—teaching Sunday school to the youngsters. Two years later, my incipient anti-colonialism was offended by the paternalistic nature of missionary work, and I just as totally and dramatically quit that church.

I matured "late," both physically and emotionally. I tend to trace the latter retardation to growing up in what, for lack of a better term, I would still call middle-class America. There was a certain provincialism. We had access neither to the vast educational resources of the high bourgeoisie nor to the street-wise practicality of the working class.

I was creative and encouraged in my creativity at home and in school. I want to pay tribute to my parents. They gave their children precious gifts of respect, honesty, a love of diversity, and the courage to question certain social expectations and created needs. We, of the next generation, were able to take these qualities further. My brother and I, particularly, have used them in developing our own—more systematic—world analyses. In turn, our parents often say they learn from us, and it's exciting that we all have grown politically as a result. My parents continue to be open to new ideas, to change; their lives are a constant reflection of it even today. And I feel the spiral ascending within my own life as I again learn from their amazing capacity to keep on moving.

My father and mother always asked questions, they informed themselves, they took us on summer trips to South America, Alaska, and Europe. They trusted us, and generally allowed us to set our own limits on where we might go and with whom, how we spent our time, how late we could stay out at night. Most importantly, they supported us in our searches: emotionally, intellectually, and also (when they felt they could) economically.

Of course the atmosphere of a fast-growing western U.S. military town also had its impact upon me. As I had briefly joined the Episcopal Church, so I briefly joined Job's Daughters,* played country and western music on the phonograph to drown out my father's Friday night string quartets of which I was ashamed (because they were "different"), tried (but failed) to be cheerleader and homecoming queen in high school. All of these essentially involved insider/outsider issues.

I dreamed of dating the captain of the football team. When I did, he raped me.

I eventually became an insider within a kind of outsider group—eggheads (today they would be called nerds) who edited the school paper, worked on the school yearbook, involved our-

* A Masonic organization for girls and young women.

selves in school theatre, took a creative writing course and produced our first poems and short stories.

This brings us to the mid-fifties. In the larger world McCarthy was bludgeoning America's creativity and courage in a way we would feel for the next twenty years. I went to college, got bored

Margaret's high school picture, Albuquerque, 1954

with it, dropped out. (Interestingly, while many women of my generation and social class had to fight to be allowed to go on to college, in my family my brother, sister, and I all were expected to do so. We were encouraged, and supported. Again—an outsider of sorts—I am the only one of the three of us who didn't get a university degree!)

I married young, just barely eighteen, probably not really understanding that I could strike out on my own by a less painful route. My first husband was spoiled, woman-hating, and charming; I became an insider as the dutiful wife who justifies her husband's shortcomings to everyone including herself.

By the time I was fed-up, I had worked at the usual female jobs—secretary, gofer, model. I divorced and moved to New York City. I was twenty-one, and knew I wanted to be a writer. The insider's way of going about that was in New York, the "literary capital of the world." Just as I had earned my first typewriter and learned to type at the age of nine, sure that was the way you did it, so I journeyed as a brave new writer to the place I believed all brave new writers had to go to break into publishing.

New York presented a whole new set of insider/outsider problems. How to support myself, and still have time for writing? I did it by working in the garment district, waiting tables, modeling for artists, working in offices. I immediately became part of an artists' world in which time for creativity was valued above all else, including consumerism and other such pieces of the American dream. And I became an insider in that outsider's world.

We prided ourselves in being reluctant to venture above Manhattan's 14th Street. On the south side of that dividing line was our loosely consolidated world: struggling artists and writers, old factories converted into affordable lofts, a dozen ways to put one over on Con Ed, job solidarity, collective gallery and publishing endeavors. On the north side were the uptown galleries, museums, and publishers—to which most of us were eager to sell out as soon as we possibly could.

Living the way I chose to live in New York City, with the particular hierarchy of values I was then acquiring, made me something of an outsider to my family. My parents had raised me with a great range of possibilities; it was difficult for them to understand why I chose to live in what they considered a slum. Independence was doggedly important to me.

I remember a visit from my father and brother—the latter was young, maybe ten, at the time. I was living on New York's lower east side, proud of my three-flight walk up with its bathtub in the kitchen and its newly patched floors. I served them a dinner that began with shrimp cocktail; it must have taken close to half my week's wage to buy the food. They hardly touched it, and their discomfort at visiting me in such a place was painful for us all.

In spite of this discomfort, though, my parents always supported their children's lives, and continue to do so—no matter how difficult it occasionally must be for them to understand why we choose to do the things we do. They were staunch allies when I became the object of my grandparents' disapproval, most notably when I decided to have Gregory. They have supported my political views, and through the last few years stood proudly by me in my struggle against deportation.

Back during those four years in New York I learned things that continue to be fundamental in my life and work. A further-ranging curiosity. Discipline. Hard work. A critical eye. And although I truly believed that I lived totally below 14th Street, and had no use or need for a larger world, in fact I was also learning my first notions of how I would eventually fit in—or not fit in—to the larger world of my times. My first real political ideas originated and were nourished in New York. I went to work for Nancy Macdonald at Spanish Refugee Aid. I marched in my first demonstration. I began my first political readings.

And I did something that marked me, absolutely, as an outsider in ways that had previously not been present in my life. I had my first child intentionally on my own, outside the context of traditional marriage.

This was 1960. For white, middle-class America—even the artists and writers of white middle-class America—you got married and had children. You might get married, have a child, and get divorced. You might even become pregnant, get married, and have a child. Or (less likely) become pregnant, have a child, and get married. You didn't believe you weren't good in relation-ships, decide you wanted a child, and set about to have one—on your own. Except that's exactly what I did.

Deciding I wasn't good in relationships, of course, had to do with a whole other aspect of the insider/outsider syndrome which would later clarify itself for many of us when feminist ideas re-emerged. Up to that time I blamed myself for what I perceived as my inability to be happy in a relationship with a man; I saw the problems as personal—mine alone—rather than social. I knew, though, that I wanted to be a mother. My strong tendency towards the outsider's position led me to charge straight ahead. I appreciated those who supported me and largely ignored those who didn't.

I gave birth to Gregory on October 14th, 1960, at old Manhat-tan General Hospital. For the next ten months I made my way with him, raising him in a time and place almost completely devoid of support systems for single mothers. Every solution to every problem involved some variety of outsider ingenuity.

Some members of my family had urged me to get an abortion, telling me I would be depriving my child of the "normal" nuclear family structure. I could see for myself that the nuclear family was no longer the norm, although at that point I probably would have been hard put to theorize about why.

Just as we artists lived off of periodic unemployment checks, learned how to turn back the hands on gas meters, and scorned all manner of comforts in order to pursue our real work, I wheeled and dealed, cajoled and invented to get my son into extraordinary one-of-a-kind day-care programs. My generation, like others, did a great deal of theorizing about arrangements which, if not better, were certainly different. I can remember periods of collective living, "smash monogamy," and even a time when certain groups maintained it was wrong to have children at all. All these ideas, each in its moment, screamed their outsider nature to mom-and-apple-pie America; each also relegated those who were somehow involved but would not follow "the line" to a position of outsider among outsiders.

Several years ago, at a party in New York City, I sat in a corner with a woman named Hettie Cohen. In the late fifties and early sixties when I lived in New York, Hettie and I had been present at many of the same gatherings; she was then married to LeRoi Jones, Black poet who would later call himself Amiri Baraka. I was beginning to think of myself as a poet, and frequented much of the same crowd. As women, we were groupies. We flitted among the male figures, wrote as much like them as we could, did their laundry, typed their manuscripts, and slept with them on their initiative. Thirty years later Hettie told me: "You coped with it by leaving; I coped with it by staying."

In late 1961, I took Gregory and went to Mexico City. I had no idea, then, that I would live outside this country for the next twenty-three years. Nor that I would experience things and make decisions—good ones and bad—that would influence the insider/outsider aspects of the rest of my life.

As a single mother in the middle class of those years I had been an outsider in my land of origin. In the land of my arrival I was even more of one. I was outsider as foreigner, outsider as woman alone with a robust infant (and it may well have been the robust condition of my infant that set me apart in Mexico, as of course the streets were filled with thousands of single mothers supporting tens of thousands of kids—few of them robust). I was outsider among the men I met: a woman who thought she could write like them, hang out with them, dream with them of intercultural exchange. And outsider, finally, because—of them all—I was the one who never doubted that I could take that dream and push it to reality.

Of course these weren't the only ways in which I was outsider, nor the only groups of people for whom this was what I was. The vague guilt, simply because I was a North American, which I had experienced years before with my first husband in Europe, returned to plague me with repeated murkiness. Identification with a government responsible for so much of the world's oppression is not an easy load to carry.

I still remember a scene in a Mexican market, not long after my arrival. My Spanish was different, I had learned it in Spain, and a woman selling me a cooking crock remarked upon it. "You're not from the city," was her comment, " . . . from the north, maybe, Monterrey . . .?" I hadn't expected that anyone would mistake my Brooklynese Spanish for the lilt of another state. "I'm not from Mexico. . ." I started to respond. But before I could finish she guessed again: "Italy, then?" And before I knew what I was doing, I nodded affirmation. "I'm from Italy," I lied to the market woman. I did not want, at that moment and for whatever complex reasons, to say I was from the United States. It was all right to be other, but not that particular other.

The relationship between Mexico and the United States was—and is—fraught with the stigmata of unequal neighbors, imperialist use, resentment, pain that twists both cultures out of shape along a meandering and battered border, grief turned in upon itself, greed, frustration. A privileged young white woman moves into that context. A load of useless guilt had weighted other areas of her life, why not this one? That was my Mexican beginning.

The Mexican years, for me, are marked most forcefully by *El Corno Emplumado/The Plumed Horn*, a bilingual literary quarterly which would be important across borders within a whole renaissance of "little" (read: independent) publishing. I founded the magazine with a Mexican poet I would also marry, Sergio Mondragon.

And so those years are marked, as well, by that marriage, by the births of my three daughters—Sarah, Ximena, Ana—and by the ways in which experiencing a Third World country from a position, if not entirely insider at least not entirely outsider, changed my world view and the way I saw myself.

There was an insider/outsider dynamic which developed around *El Corno*. From the beginning, Sergio edited the Spanish side, I the English. My inability to trust myself with literature in a language not my own prevented me from pushing for a less dichotomized, more truly collective working relationship. Sergio did his best to keep me believing I could never edit in Spanish. But our political visions diverged, as did many of our ideas about literature, and after six years, Sergio left the magazine. I continued to edit its last few issues, and managed perfectly well with the Spanish; after all, I had by then been living and functioning almost a decade in that language. Later, in Havana, I would move much farther in my Spanish language skills: judging literary contests, and eventually writing books. But I'm getting ahead of myself.

I lived in Mexico from 1961 through 1969. From the beginning, I attempted to ameliorate the loneliness, intensified by the brand of sexism I'd faced in New York, by being a "good girl." I could marry (again), suffer my husband's particular distortions with a grace that belied my "castrating American womanhood" (his term); I could do more than anyone on earth: be wife and mother, work, write, run a magazine, be an international bridge, and thereby make myself a necessity; I could be more faithful, more loyal, more subservient, more "Mexican."

In 1967, I even became a Mexican citizen. A lawyer, who had little if any knowledge of how that act would eventually affect my life, told me I would be able to obtain a better job, which at that point we sorely needed. Looking back, I wonder if this might not have been symptomatic as well of the way I tended to take things on from the time I was a child: all out and completely. The bridge didn't want to feel she had been imposed by the Alliance for Progress or A.I.D. She wanted to feel as if she had been constructed, stone by stone, reed by reed, by Mexican as well as American hands.

At the same time as I reconstructed myself to "fit in," however, I was constructing and reconstructing myself in other dimensions which would eventually permit me to push beyond the choices that are presented to us and say *there are other options.* In Mexico I became part of an international group of writers and artists who had never been flattened into the cookie-molds of art disconnected from life. The poets I met and learned from, whatever their individual voices, inherited the passion and commitment of a Cesar Vallejo, a Violeta Parra.

I became a midwife in the misery belt around one of the poorest and fastest-growing cities in the world (seventeen million at last count). That experience brought me back to my womanhood in ways I am only now beginning to interpret. It also brought up insider/outsider issues, particularly in terms of race. I remember a beautiful Zapotec woman whose baby I had just delivered telling me, "This makes eleven mouths to feed, but I'd gladly have another if it was blond and blue-eyed—like yours."

The 1968 Mexican student movement taught me both the power of protest and the lengths to which a repressive government will go to kill that protest off.

Two trips to Cuba—one to a meeting of poets in 1967, the other to a meeting of Third World intellectuals the following year—also opened new avenues of possibility for my life.

Feminism, as theory and collectivity, moved me deeply when it filtered down from the North American movement late in 1968. If it seems, Ruth, that I'm running much too fast over events and directions which were fundamental in my life, it's because the story is a long one and, in this letter at least, I don't want to get waylaid. I feel the need to focus most specifically on those ideas and moments which most heavily impacted my identity as insider and/or outsider.

I've written in a number of places about the Mexican years, and how they ended. Quickly, then: problems originating in my participation in the student movement of the year before forced me into hiding and finally out of the country in 1969. Publishing the magazine had become impossible. Sergio and I had separated in 1967, and I had begun living with the U.S. poet Robert Cohen. We had had my fourth child and she was three months old when the repression hit. She, her brother of eight and her two sisters, then five and four, traveled to Cuba several months before I was finally able to make the trip.

Linked to these events was another insider/outsider toll-station, so to speak. Still in hiding, I asked my parents if they would take my children until I could resolve the situation. My mother, overwhelmed by it all, wrote me a letter neither of us has forgotten. She refused, commenting that I should have considered my politics when deciding to have children, or considered having children, given my politics.

I replied that my politics had essentially given me the courage to have children, and that my children—among other considerations—informed my politics by making me very desperately want to help create a different world for them, and for all children.

Who knows how different my life—or my children's—might have been had my mother taken them instead of responding as she did. I probably would not have gone to live in Cuba, for one thing. I have no regrets about that move, though. Quite the contrary. Much as it continues to complicate my life today.

I went to Cuba. I lived there, with Robert for six years, without him for five more. I had published two small anthologies in Mexico, one about the Hippie movement, the other on women's liberation as it had begun to evolve in the United States. In Cuba I began my involvement with oral history. I began to experience the voices of those who had been kept voiceless as something necessary to my own work. By now I considered myself a feminist, later also an oral historian. And I didn't come to that discipline from the academy, but as I came to most things which have been important in my life: through searching, finding, and learning along the way.

From 1969 to 1980—when I went to Nicaragua to live—I wrote more than a dozen books. A few were poetry, there were some essays, there was translation; but most of this work was oral history, and most of it centered on women. I became a vehicle for the voices of Cuban women, Peruvian women, Chilean women, Nicaraguan women, women from other parts of Latin America, a Puerto Rican woman, women from Vietnam.

By virtue of their poverty, exploitation, illiteracy, and female oppression, these women were truly outsiders. My bringing them inside, making it possible for them to be heard, and their permitting that, their decision to speak, changed their lives and my own. Trusting and using my privilege, these women became more insider as they were heard. I also became more of an insider as I drew closer to my fundamental calling. My role as a bridge acquired a new dimension, my feminism became more complex, more solid, and I moved closer to what would be an essential place in my creative personhood.

Within their communities, the women whose testimony I gathered also in some cases became more outsiders. They acquired a voice their sisters didn't have. In some instances they took on the responsibility of (and criticism implicit in) speaking for those

44

sisters. And they opened themselves to the possibility of being misunderstood, or even used, by the broader world.

I also became more of an outsider, in the eyes of conventional society; one, because I lived and worked in places like Cuba and Nicaragua. Two, because I engaged in an academic discipline— oral history—that is itself suspect in establishment eyes. And three, because I chose to listen to *women's* voices—claiming them, honoring them, giving importance to their vision. A feminist stance is still an outsider's stance in our society, and it is particularly despised by those who fear the loss of their ill-gotten power.

My relationship with my homeland also underwent intense changes during those years abroad.

I was constantly in touch with what was happening here. My contacts with those who were in the midst of all kinds of struggles may even have been more varied and in some ways more intense than if I had remained in the United States. My home was an almost obligatory stopover for Latin Americans traveling north and North Americans traveling south. This was true especially for those on their way to Cuba, and later Nicaragua.

El Corno Emplumado had exchange subscriptions with almost every little magazine anywhere. I talked and listened, was a part of the discussions of those times, kept up with what was happening. And I traveled. I went to the States, and also Canada, not only to visit my family but on lengthy reading and lecture tours in 1964, 1966, 1975, 1978, 1983. On one of these trips I spoke on seventy U.S. campuses in a period of three and a half months.

In terms of a national identity, then, I remained a North American. It was North American women I felt I represented when I attended international forums, or spoke with other women in the Amazonian jungle or the liberated zones of South Vietnam. And I have every reason to believe my North American sisters saw me, as well, as representing them in these contexts. But I was also someone whose identity was informed—culturally, socially, politically—by living in Latin America, experiencing Marxism in Spanish, and raising her children under socialism. These facts of my life, simple when listed in this letter, made me very much an insider or very much an outsider, depending on the angle from which I might be judged.

The insider/outsider dilemma in my writing had at least something to do with my engagement with photography in 1979. I produced literature in Spanish, continued to write poetry in English, and was surrounded by colleagues and friends—even my own children—who could not bridge the language barrier (fusion?) in my work. A good deal of my work had been translated, but I was never really happy with the way that came off.

Perhaps I wanted a language that would obviate words. I don't know. Photography has its own language, and mine developed its version of that early on, so this is not something I usually dwell on when speaking about how I began to make pictures. I do so here, because the implications may shed further light on the variety of insider/outsider dilemmas in my work.

In the photography itself, I have felt both insider and outsider. Insider, because I lived in places and at times when history was being made. Important history. History I could chronicle in my pictures. Outsider, because I came to photography late—in my forties—and because I learned the craft not in a school but apprenticed to a willing teacher in Cuba where we sometimes shot dozens of "rolls" with an empty camera, because we had no film.

A great deal could be written about that decade in Cuba. I hope to write a book about it one day. It was such an important time in Cuban history, and such an important time in my life. When I moved to Cuba the revolution was already ten years old. The initial decisions had been made; some of their fruits were already being reaped, and some mistakes were also being recognized.

I came from the country that had most determinedly attempted to destroy the Cuban revolution, had attacked the island innumerable times, launched overt and covert actions against it, set up an economic blockade and influenced other countries to cooperate with it in trying to sink that brave experiment ninety miles from U.S. shores. Yet I was not treated as an outsider by the Cubans. On the other hand, by my own people, I have many times been treated as one simply for having lived in Cuba.

46

Margaret during a session of the Photographer's Union, Havana, Cuba, 1979. (Photo: Grandal)

And throughout that decade I was insider/outsider in many more subtle ways. In spite of living geographically close to my family and friends of origin, politics made communication difficult. Mail travels to Czechoslovakia on its way between Cuba and the United States (airmail letters take a month), phone calls are often impossible, telegrams problematic. My parents had to defy the State Department when they wanted to visit their grand-children. My children had to go through Lima the first time they visited their grandparents.

Then there was the nature of life itself. Feminist struggles had not yet become prominent in Cuba. Engaging in those struggles on our own, Robert and I often felt very much alone. On the other hand, the socialist state took responsibility for day care, education, people's health, recreation, culture. Raising four children, it was easier to do my writing because the society in which I lived helped with their care.

Living in a country building socialism opened insider/out-sider questions most notably with regard to class. One of the most important aspects of my children's education was, I think, the way Cuban schools combine intellectual and manual labor from the earliest years. In her day care, my daughter Ana was taken to the factories where the little tables they sat at were made, where the small cups they drank their milk from were fashioned. Seeing these productive processes, getting to know the workers who made those items for them, the children gained a healthy respect for people who make things; the beginnings of a producer rather than a consumer mentality.

When they were old enough, the kids raised their own fruits and vegetables in school plots. And beginning with junior high, students combined their studies with field or factory work in much more significant ways. In Cuba, my son and daughters grew up with as much familiarity with planting potatoes and harvesting coffee as they had with the workings of a scientific laboratory or the literary classics. This broke down insider/outsider categories for them and, through them, to a certain extent, for me.

Those were years of transition for the revolution. When we went to Cuba, food rationing was acute. Foreigners, never expected by the Cubans to live as they themselves were forced to, were assigned different—better—ration books. We (and one other foreign family I knew) refused the special rations. We wanted to be insiders, at least insofar as the sacrifices were concerned. Of course we could never be so completely. For we weren't obliged to build our family as additions in the housing occupied by one set or another of our own parents. The Cubans allotted us an apartment. And when we left, we did so obeying the demands or inclinations of our lives; free to come and go, not having to betray or turn our backs on anything.

In spite of the fact that leaving Cuba and going to Nicaragua marked, in many ways, the beginning of a whole other period, another place, another chapter in my life, there are ways in which I now see the move to Nicaragua as the beginning of my coming home.

Technically speaking, for the first time in many years I was traveling with a passport that matched my acquired citizenship. Because, after much struggle over an eleven-year period, the Mexican government finally reissued my papers. (The original theft in 1969 was carried out by paramilitary operatives; the Mexican government always claimed they had nothing to do with it. But they did not, until 1979, provide me with a new passport, even though most of the people imprisoned or exiled as a result of the 1968 events had long since been amnestied.) Although, as I say, I always thought of myself as North American at heart, having a travel document from wherever was important to a logistical insiderness.

Something was beginning in Nicaragua. The Sandinistas had come to power only months before I arrived for the first time (in late 1979, for three months, to gather material for *Sandino's Daughters*), and much was new. Perhaps coming to something new is always a little like coming home.

At the same time I assumed an outsider's role in my family. I had always lived with my children, with the exception of those brief months in 1969 waiting to get out of Mexico. I was very tangibly their center pin, the person who held them together, the constant reference point for my son and daughters. I lived with different men at different periods of time; two of them were blood-fathers to three of the children. But they came and went. I remained. Until my move to Nicaragua.

By late 1980, my kids were twenty, seventeen, sixteen, and eleven. I had been living, for the previous five years, with Antonio Castro, a Colombian poet and musician. I recognized my need to leave. I recognized my need to move on, to Nicaragua, to do that no matter what. I spoke with my children, letting each of them know he or she was welcome to accompany me on the next lap of the journey. Only to Ana, my youngest, I offered no options; she would come with me since she was too young—I believed—for anything else.

Gregory had almost finished college and was already living with the woman who would become his wife. Sarah was also getting her engineering degree. Both of them opted to remain in Cuba. Ximena also wanted to stay, at least until she finished high school. When she did, the following year, she came to live with us in Nicaragua. Antonio would have followed me; it was I who eventually decided—as I had so many times before—that the relationship had played itself out. Antonio and I have retained a closeness over the years that withstood even that uneven wrenching. And I'm glad for it.

The Nicaraguan years began—for Ana and for me—with fresh insider/outsider considerations.

I had known many of the Sandinistas in Cuba, was not completely an outsider among them. I had already written two books dealing with their struggle and, in fact, the second of these developed from an invitation to "come and talk to our women" from my old friend Ernesto Cardenal, poet involved in the inception of *El Corno Emplumado*, Catholic priest, now Nicaragua's Minister of Culture. I was also less of an outsider because, as I've said, so much was new. When people begin to build something huge, like their lives, everyone in on the ground floor somehow assumes an equality in the collective work.

For Ana there were many insider/outsider issues. Raised in socialism, I still remember her horror and confusion the first time she saw a child begging in the street. In Nicaragua, kids her age were quite literally soldiers; many had fought in the recent war, many had lost family. In Cuba children are "the spoiled ones of the revolution"—they enjoy advantages not yet available to everyone. Ana's relationship to kids in her class at school, kids who were to become her friends, often involved totally new dimensions for her.

I worked at the Ministry of Culture, and later with the media. I continued to be interested in the roles women were playing, and the ways poetry, photography, and other arts were considered essential in the construction of a healthy, healing society. And I wrote. I began to be interested in the role Christians had played in making the revolution, and the one they played in the new Nicaragua. My next project would be a book about this phenomenon: the coming together, in a visible, practical way, of socialism and Christianity.

Here, again, I began as an outsider. I was not a believer, not a Christian, yet I wanted to understand the Christian stance in this revolution, what effect the armed struggle had on these people and what effect they, Christians, had on what was happening in Nicaragua. Because of my lack of religious belief, I was wary of assuming a patronizing position when writing about the theological aspects of this phenomenon. I asked an Italian priest (who specialized in the study of atheism!) to work with me.

But as I moved from feeling outsider to feeling insider—without necessarily altering my belief system—I realized I didn't need to involve him in the writing. He understood, and I went on by myself. My deep connection to people in the Nicaraguan Church has continued long after *Christians in the Nicaraguan Revolution** was published there and here; what I learned in that experience remains and grows in my ever-expanding sense of self.

Death. I need to talk about death, Ruth, and the role it has assumed in my life. It was in Cuba that I first began to experience the sudden deaths of people close to me, men and women whose physical lives went out in the rigors of that terribly uneven struggle for people's freedom.

Roque Dalton's death marked me. He and I had been close for years; he was tortured to death by fanatic members of his own organization in El Salvador in 1975. Rodolfo Walsh's death marked me. When paramilitary squads in Argentina killed his daughter, he used his journalist's skills to write an open letter exposing the death squads as coming from the three branches of the dictatorship's armed forces. He was disappeared a couple of days later and never found. José Benito Escobar's death marked me. My last memory of him in Cuba goes back to the time he trudged up nine flights of stairs with two new mattresses for my kids' beds. We knew him as "Alvaro." An infiltrator working for the CIA earned one

* *Christians in the Nicaraguan Revolution* by Margaret Randall. Vancouver, B.C., Canada: New Star Books, 1983.

51

thousand dollars in U.S. currency for turning him in. These and many many other friends left like this.

In Nicaragua my proximity to this kind of death continued. Only there it was suddenly something I shared with an entire nation. Of a population of three million, fifty thousand had died in the war against Somoza. Forty thousand children became orphans. When I arrived in Nicaragua the first time—to work on the book about women—people were just beginning to open the graves of sons, daughters, other family members who had been buried where they fell. Their bodies were being moved to cemeteries. Is one more insider or more outsider sitting on the edge of the waiting coffin while relatives, their mouths and noses covered with handkerchiefs, dig for the paltry remains of a loved one? How to speak of the insider/outsider syndrome in this context?

Nicaragua, as a nation, also occupies a peculiarly poignant position with relation to the United States. The Reagan administration has defined Nicaragua as communist and totalitarian, when in fact it knows the Sandinistas are attempting to build a pluralist, mixed economy, with ideological input from socialists, Christian democrats, liberation theologians, and others. Reagan personally goes to absurd lengths when referring to the "freedom fighters" and proudly proclaims himself a contra.

In calling Nicaragua communist, the U.S. government hopes to cancel it out, by simple labeling prevent anyone from taking a careful look at this new and vital experiment. And, as we currently witness, the Reagan government will go to any lengths to destroy that experiment, including breaking its own laws and going against its own Congress. This is an example of an administration deciding a country is outside, no matter what lies it must tell, what outrages it must commit to do so.

Consequently, the administration also labels as outsiders U.S. citizens and others who get in the way of these lies. For several years now, North Americans traveling to Nicaragua have been subject to illegal searches, their possessions confiscated and papers copied upon their return. FBI agents have visited their workplaces, spoken to their supervisors, tendered all manner of subtle and not so subtle threats simply because the person in question has exercised his or her right to travel. And a bill has recently been introduced into Congress which, if passed, would make it illegal to travel to Nicaragua at all.

Ben Linder, a U.S. citizen working as a technician in that country's northern mountains, was cold-bloodedly murdered by the contras in April of 1987, and the administration carried out its own private investigation but refuses to address the issue. I am sure my own years in Nicaragua and my writing about that country have a great deal to do with the U.S. Immigration Service's denial of my residency. If we are curious about a country not in favor with the current administration, if we visit that country, speak or write about it, plead for nonintervention in its internal affairs, we are outsiders. And for the Reagan administration, the line between outsider and traitor is frighteningly tenuous.

And then there's the whole business of coming home. The return to this country. The recognitions and the shocks. That first year, how I worked to preserve the sights and sounds in *Albuquerque: Coming Back to the USA.** And of course there's the INS case which, perhaps because it is so close, is the hardest to write about.

I returned to this country in January of 1984. I returned to Albuquerque, the city where I grew up and where my parents and brother live. Floyce Alexander was important in this picture. We had known one another for years and had begun a lover relationship when I visited my family in 1983. When I was sure I wanted to live here, Floyce and I married. We petitioned for my permanent residency. I wanted to recover my citizenship—if, in fact, I had really lost it. (That question has yet to go to its final legal appeal.)

I saw—and see—myself as a woman at midlife, returning after twenty-three years in Latin America to the place where I grew up, where my family is. I see myself as someone in search of my roots, but bringing with me on that search the varied experiences, the rich cultural connections made and preserved from those other places. I was tired when I came home. I wanted time and space to contemplate the pieces of my life, understand how they might fit together, use them in the ongoing construction of a whole.

* *Albuquerque: Coming Back to the USA* by Margaret Randall. Vancouver, B.C., Canada: New Star Books, 1986.

Insider/outsider issues have been powerfully present, from the beginning.

At first I felt very much outside. Much was familiar, yet it was difficult for me to frequent shopping malls, enter large department stores, figure out what I might do to earn a living. I felt that I had a great deal to give, but wasn't sure how to give it. All manner of things—from progress made in the struggle against racism to the workings of a money machine—startled and amazed me.

I also felt inside. Inside, in that I made certain connections, saw a certain history, changes that had been struggled for and in some instances won, in ways I felt those who had remained here could not see; they were too close.

The three and a half years since my return have held their share of insider/outsider problems.

INS decided to deny me residency and order me deported, based on the content of my writings.

I began to teach at the University of New Mexico and found: one, that I love teaching, and two, that I am almost always at odds with the institutional system. I have had extraordinary support from students, colleagues, department chairs, and even some in the school's administration; but my lack of an academic degree (in spite of fifty published books) and my current political problems make me an outsider to the insiders and more than commonly vulnerable to indignities and uncertainties.

The INS case itself is fundamentally an insider/outsider situation. To be threatened with the loss of one's family and one's place because of one's ideas is a threat to one's basic identity.

In choosing to assume this battle—for myself and for others—I place myself in a continuing drama in which my insider/outsider pieces must do battle with one another.

This battle has become a constant. It is most raw before immigration judges and when questioned by red-baiting womanizing government lawyers. Or with the press, giving interviews and statements one knows may be distorted or taken out of context. Or on talk shows where listeners calling in often tell me to "go back where you came from." Or on the street when someone approaches, suddenly, and I never know if he or she will lash out or offer support. Or in a classroom where I must assume someone is sitting in for Accuracy in Academia. Or on the level of simplest personal exchange when so many of the energies of family, loved ones, colleagues, and friends are exhausted helping to carry this load.

Floyce and I separated. We are close, as we have been since we met. Perhaps we should have remained friends instead of trying to be lovers. Yet our most intimate time together was important for us both. For me, the deep devotion and commitment on both sides were an essential part of my homecoming. We came together at extremely lonely, needful, and vulnerable times in our lives. Ultimately our very different needs and lifestyles couldn't weather my speed-of-light journey.

I discovered an incest experience in my infancy, and took on, as well, the task of working it through, writing about it, and publishing a book which uses poetry, prose, and photographic images to reveal the process of that experience. I have also read these incest poems and continue to read them in theaters, halls, women's bookstores, and elsewhere across the country. Each of these readings is a powerful insider/outsider experience for me, and most often, afterwards, scores of people—mostly women—come up and tell me how my sharing has affected their memory of their own histories of abuse. Feminist therapy helped me get to the point of being able to write *This is About Incest,** and continues to help me live my life.

My first immigration hearing, four days in El Paso, Texas, was a frightening and affirming event. I was an outsider there, in the eyes of the government, before the hearing started and when it was finished. In fact, the basic intent of the prosecuting lawyers was to make me look guilty by virtue of being outside. Exploring my beliefs and my commitment to those beliefs—as well as simply my right to hold beliefs of any kind—was basic to the maintenance of my dignity. And in holding onto that dignity I became more and more an insider to myself.

My children live in four different countries; two of them will

* *This is About Incest* by Margaret Randall. Ithaca, NY: Firebrand Books, 1987.

soon be parents themselves.* So this case, with its attendant situation of my not being able to leave and re-enter this country until my appeals are exhausted will separate me from my grandchildren as it does from my children. Living next door to my own parents, as they live out their last years, situates me precisely between those who brought me to this life and those I brought to it. There are insider/outsider lessons here, as well.

Half of my life has been lived in the United States, the country in which I was born. Almost the other half in Latin America: in Mexico, Cuba, and finally Nicaragua. I have been, alternately and in many different ways, a stranger in my children's land, witness, participant, insider, outsider, and finally—back in the land of my birth—a cultural hybrid still in search of my fullest identity.

National cultures and landscapes, language and custom, were not the only variables. Different political systems also made a weave out of this process in my life. In the United States, I grew up and came to womanhood in an over-industrialized capitalist country. In Mexico, I came to know dependent capitalism. In Cuba, socialism. And in Nicaragua, a new experiment in political pluralism: Sandinism, socialism, Christianity. In my relationship to each of these places, and within whatever context I experienced them, the insider/outsider syndrome took on new meaning in my life.

Ruth, there is so much more I could write. And I want to respond to much that was in your first letter as well (I'll do that as we go along.) These last few years, especially, have been ripe with connections, new ways of seeing myself and those around me, new ideas about all that continues to be important in my life.

Much love,

Margaret

---

* My son Gregory and his wife Laura gave birth to their daughter Lia Margarita on October 7, 1987. My daughter Ximena and her husband Fito gave birth to their son Luis Rodrigo on February 10, 1988.

My most insider space is with people

Letter Four

Woods Hole, Massachusetts
August 2nd, 1987

Dearest Margaret:

Today I want to sketch out my life, as background for the thoughts I am having about how insider/outsider dynamics touch on my experiences as a woman, mother, wife, scientist, Jew, and many others. So, I'll start at the beginning and try to touch on the main decision points.

My earliest memories are of feeling inside, comfortable in and with my family. I was born in the heyday of my parents' marriage and was very much a wanted child. My mother used to say that the main reason she married was to have children and I took that to mean, to have me. My father later became very busy with his work as a doctor. When I was born he had just opened his practice and had lots of time for me. My parents had been fellow medical students and residents at the Vienna General Hospital, but after I arrived, my mother stopped working at medicine and stayed home for a while. Later she got quite sick with a mysterious neurological illness and then went back to work, but only with my father, never again on her own.

Ruth and her parents, Vienna, 1927

My father was heart and soul Viennese and enjoyed showing me the parts of Vienna that he loved especially. My mother had come as a child from Galicia (the Polish part of the Austro-Hungarian empire before World War I) and always felt like something of an outsider in Vienna. Perhaps partly for this reason, she kept me apart from other children. She focused it on "germs," her particular physician's mania—avoiding illness. She or our maid took me for walks to the nearby park and played with me. (We always had at least one live-in maid, even when my parents were poor; part of the Austrian class structure which brought large numbers of young women from the countryside into the city to work as domestics for little more than bed and board.) But I never played with other children. Yet I could see other children playing together.

What's more, I had lots of cousins my age because my father had six siblings, but I hardly knew them even though all of us lived in Vienna. There was the clear sense that we were different from the others. My father liked only one brother and one sister and disliked the rest. And although he and my mother participated in family occasions out of respect for his parents, they kept me and my younger brother away. So, although we were insiders to each other, a "close" family, we were sort of outsiders to the larger family. My father translated his alienation into a sense of superiority, based on a number of grounds—political (he was a socialist, they were bourgeois), religious (he was an atheist, they were irreligious but traditional), professional (he a physician, they business people). Also he was married to a professional woman, while he thought of his brothers' wives as "bridge-playing housewives." All those distinctions were implicit if not explicit, and I took them in.

My mother has said that it was important to her that I grow up thinking the world to be reasonable and predictable. She made it a point to answer my questions and explain all rules, so there wouldn't be any mysterious do's and don'ts. And it is true that I grew up expecting whatever happens to have reasons and that I could find out what they were. This may be one reason why I am a scientist and part of my sense of at-homeness in nature.

Later, especially after my brother was born, my family itself developed an insider/outsider dynamic, with me and my father the insiders (at least to me) and my mother and brother, the outsiders. By the time my brother was two years old, he had become a very kvetchy kid. My father now was busy and the typical husband/father, who came home late and tired and wanted to relax, not parent. He and I would go on Sunday expeditions, while my mother stayed home with my brother. Later, when my brother got bigger, he'd come "with us" and my mother still usually stayed home because by then she had headaches, gallstones, other ailments. I felt closely identified with my father, who was the center of power, the insider, in the family.

Just before I started first grade, my mother had my hair bobbed in a short boy's haircut. The boyish haircut was in style among progressive women as a protest against the impracticality of traditional, elaborately "feminine" hairdos, but mine was startlingly short. This created no problems in my girls' grammar school where gender wasn't an issue, but I also entered the coed Children's Conservatory, with classes in piano, English, and gymnastics. The first day in gym class, where everyone wore shorts and T-shirts, the teacher asked girls to sit on one side of the room and boys on the other (why?). I was reprimanded for sitting with the girls, since the teacher and, I suppose, the other children took me to be a boy. An odd outsiderish way to start school.

I went to grammar school within walking distance of where both sets of my grandparents and many of my aunts and uncles lived. What's more, it was the school my father had gone to. So, in a sense, very insider. But by then my father's practice had picked up and we had more money than most of my classmates. Also, my parents were professionals and actively supported the social-democratic government of Austria and the militantly socialist city government of Vienna that was trying to expand social services in the face of economic depression. Most of the other parents owned or worked in small shops and were apolitical or bourgeois-middle-of-the-road. I was politically aware and therefore different from my classmates. I was also usually the "best" student and teacher's pet. We had books at home, went to concerts and plays. So, I was also outsider.

In February 1934, when I was just short of ten, the Austrian fascists staged a coup against the elected government. I spent the next days at home, under curfew, listening to radio reports of government losses against a background of machine gun fire. As a physician, my father was allowed to move about and would come home with stories of barbed wire strung across the bridges a block from our house, about shelling of the model workers' apartments which the workers and their families were trying to defend. After three days of fighting, the government fell. Since my parents were opposed to the fascists, I knew that I must not talk politics in school because a wrong word in the wrong place could send them to jail. But beyond that my life didn't change much, until four years later, when in March 1938, a week after my fourteenth birthday, the Nazis took over.

I spent that afternoon and much of the night glued to the radio. About midnight a cable arrived from a Viennese friend, now in New York: Affidavits on the way to emigrate to the United States; register with the American Consulate; letter follows. Next morning when I woke up, storm troopers with swastika arm-bands were riding their motorcycles outside my window. The Nazis were in Vienna and I was a dirty Jew.

We had never been outside Austria. Didn't have passports. But suddenly we were going to New York. Where was New York? We had studied Africa in geography, but not yet America.

The Nazis began picking up Jews on the street. Making them scrub the sidewalks. Jeering them as they scrubbed on hands and knees. Taking them away. Where? My parents were in danger any time they left the house, but they were also in danger at home. SS and SA men (elite guards and storm troopers) were entering apartments, rounding up socialists, communists, Jews, hauling off the men and sometimes the women. We burned all suspicious-looking books in the living room stove: Marx, Engels, Lenin, Trotsky, Rosa Luxemburg, Brecht, Agnes Smedley, Thomas and Heinrich Mann, and lots more. Thank goodness we hadn't converted to central heating like so many of our friends!

Because I was a child, it was less dangerous for me to go out than for my parents. So, I got to run a lot of errands. Fun! For years I had been wandering about Vienna by myself. The narrow, cobbled streets of the Inner City were home to me, the way American kids feel about their block or their neighborhood. I felt part of the city, it part of me. But no more. Now I had to leave—quick.

After a few weeks when school reopened everything was changed. I had been a leader. Good at academics, good at sports, with lots of friends. But several of my friends weren't Jewish. Could we risk talking to each other? All of us felt tentative. Nobody said much. The teachers we had suspected of being underground Nazis now had swastikas proudly pinned to their chests. So had some we never imagined were Nazis. Jewish teachers were gone. So were half-Jews, some of whom we'd never thought of as Jewish. Soon Jewish and "Aryan" students weren't allowed to sit next to each other: Christians by the window, Jews by the door.

In July we emigrated. My parents, brother, and I. My many relatives stayed behind. Once we got out, we would help them leave. A solemn promise—to them, to ourselves. We had brand new passports with swastikas on the cover and inside, a J for Jew. We also had brand new clothes because there was no telling when we'd have money to buy clothes in America. We could take only ten marks (about two dollars) with us. The rest of our money we spent or gave to friends, so we wouldn't have to leave it to the Nazis. My father planned to stop in Italy, Switzerland, France, England, wherever he knew people who might be willing to lend him money. Once we got to the States he would have to take medical boards before he could earn anything.

We boarded the night train for Trieste where friends had invited us to stop for a few days. My parents booked all our tickets in Vienna, so we were traveling first class. Might as well travel in style, we who now had no money and had never been abroad. We reached the border at midnight. Customs agents, swastikas on their uniforms, stamped our passports. We were out of Austria! A few minutes later, Italian immigration stopped us. No staying in Italy. Straight on to Switzerland or back to Austria. My father became stubborn. He wanted to say goodbye to his friends and try to borrow money. Under guard, we were put on the next train back to the Austrian side of the border. Terrifying. I felt sick. Next morning my father phoned his friends and they promised to meet us at the Italian immigration point. This time it worked. We were out!

A month later we sailed into New York, my brother and I on deck as we passed the Statue of Liberty glowing in the sunrise. Beautiful and exciting. We moved into a tiny, one-room apartment on 72nd Street, surrounded by recent refugees. My brother and I began to roam the streets, shop, cook. In Vienna we had cooks and nursemaids. Here we were on our own. Soon my father decided there were too many refugee doctors in New York. That it would be better to settle elsewhere. He had an introduction to a physician in Boston, and went to look the situation over. The next day he called and told us to come.

Was the move away from the majority of refugees a way to be an outsider, or did my father think it would make it easier to become an insider among Americans, the real inside? I think the latter. And though he remained a self-conscious outsider, he did make many American friends, which the refugees in New York had little opportunity to do.

As soon as we arrived in Boston, my brother and I started school. I had been looking forward to going to an American high school, coeducational and with choice among different subjects, but ended up at the only all girls' public school in Boston, modeled on the European plan, with a prescribed curriculum including Latin and Greek. It was confining and uninteresting and I hated it. Hated being a foreigner in it. Refused to speak until my English got better. But I found my first friend, a refugee who had emigrated from Berlin four years earlier. We talked for hours and remained friends for life.

I cut school a lot. My mother was disoriented and depressed and liked me to stay home. That way we could go shopping together and learn our way around the neighborhood. My father spent all his time holed up with a Viennese colleague, studying for the medical boards.

November 9th, 1938: *Kristallnacht* (Night of Broken Glass). All over Germany and Austria storm troopers smashed the windows of Jewish shops and homes. Burned the synagogues to the ground. Twenty thousand Jewish men were arrested and taken to concentration camps. A week later a letter arrived from my mother's mother, still in Vienna: the temple two houses down the street was gone; her brother and his son taken away. A few days later the wives got postcards telling them their husbands were dead. My mother insisted my grandmother must leave at once! But no way for her to join us. She was born in Austrian Poland and U.S. immigration laws limited the number of people born in eastern Europe who could come in. She and others like her could register at the American consulate, but no chance that their applications would be considered till years hence. They didn't have years to wait! The Nazis were killing them right then. Quickly, my mother arranged for my grandmother to join relatives in London.

In January 1939 our furniture arrived from Vienna and we moved into an unfurnished apartment in Brookline, a suburb of Boston with a predominantly middle-class population and many Jews. A great boon for me because it let me transfer to a coed high school where I could choose my subjects. I also skipped a grade.

At Brookline High I met another German refugee with whom I became friends, but I could not relate to American girls at all. They were into clothes, make-up, dates, boyfriends. I, for my part, was trying to figure out what had hit me. Scoured the public library for magazine articles and books about Austrian and German history since World War I. Exchanged letters with Viennese friends, in Vienna or in exile. In my head I was living in Vienna more than in Brookline.

September 3rd, 1939 the Germans invaded Poland, the start of the European phase of World War II. The States were not yet in it, but we were, my parents and I. An aunt put my father's mother on a plane from Vienna to London to join one of her daughters and a grandson. In her eighties and confused, she died a few weeks later, not understanding what had happened or where she was. My parents made their final, desperate efforts to get the rest of our relatives and friends out of Vienna before the borders closed. In the end, only my father's oldest, and favorite, brother got stuck, with his wife and daughter. He was severely disabled, in a wheelchair, and unable to care for himself. As far as we know, the Nazis shipped them off to the camps, affidavits and tickets to the States in hand. That is the last I know about my favorite cousin.

Until a year before, I knew no one outside Austria. Suddenly I had relatives on four continents.

Thinking back on this time, I am sure that a major change of scene, like emigration, is especially hard for adolescents. Harder than for younger children or people in their twenties. Because at that point we are trying to figure out who we are and who we are going to be, terribly unsure of ourselves. Our identity depends on having friends and being like them. And suddenly we don't know anyone, don't speak the language, look different, dress different, are total outsiders. And the youngsters among whom we land stick to each other, and feel threatened by someone different from them. I wanted to make friends to whom I could tell my story. They didn't want to hear my story; they wanted to tell me about Saturday night's date. Most of my classmates had never heard of Austria and thought I had come from Australia.

I think this is why I and my age group lost our accents so quickly, much more quickly than younger kids or grown-ups, to at least sound like the others. To begin with, being an outsider was agony, then I became snobbish about it ("those silly girls, with nothing but boys and clothes on their minds"), then I tried to find a place among the grown-ups—my parents and their refugee friends. Finally, I did what so many children of immigrants do: I tried to distance myself from my parents and become American-ized. Senior year in high school, I began to make American friends, got a permanent wave (my only one!), bought the right clothes and shoes, became involved in the French Club and other extra-curricular activities, and got ready to graduate and go to college.

The summer between high school and college I had an inter-esting insider/outsider experience. It was also a very stimulating experience, intellectually and emotionally, that made me enter college feeling very high. I lived on a farm in a small village in Vermont with a friend from Vienna, now living in New York and three of her school friends—two German refugees and Jane, an American girl. Jane's mother had died; her father remarried, didn't want her and moved to the midwest. She was living with an aunt she hated. She was president of her school's American Student Union, an organization close to the Communist Party, and had already had one "nervous breakdown." (Later Jane was diagnosed as manic-depressive and spent much of her life in mental hospitals.) The reason I am telling you all this is to say that we were not your typical, all-American high school graduates.

The five of us arrived in Vermont equipped with books by Spinoza, Freud, Alfred North Whitehead, James Joyce, Oscar Wilde, Virginia Woolf, Vernon Parrington (a leftist American historian of that time), Nehru, Karen Horney, and I don't remember who else, that we passed around among ourselves. We read and talked endlessly, hiked up mountains, and hitchhiked in pairs all over Vermont. We took up with a family of down and out poor folk who lived in a tar-paper shack down the road and bought toys and candy for their many children. It was the summer of 1941 and in the news we were following the Germans advance into the Soviet Union. We considered ourselves socialists, but lived among staunch Republicans who thought of Roosevelt's New Deal as communism. It was very much an insider/outsider experience: we were a very cohesive group—all women, with tentative Lesbian feelings but no explicit sexuality, and lots of fantasies about our sexual and marital futures—insiders among ourselves, but complete outsiders among the people with whom we were living. We hayed and went to grange suppers, but the farmer and his wife didn't know what to make of us and always introduced us as "the girls from New York," perhaps a euphemism for "from the moon."

That fall I entered Radcliffe, the women's college of Harvard, but continued to live at home. I made new friends, but given the choice—and Radcliffe offered that choice—most of them were refugees from the Nazis or the war, French, Czech, English, German, Chinese. The only American-born member of our circle of friends was a Black woman from Atlanta, whose mother had come with her, I believe because it was impossible for her to get a room in the dorms! Interestingly, all my women friends were foreigners, but my male friends, except for a long-time friend from Vienna, were American. That may reflect the fact that my female friendships went deeper than my friendships with men, but I think it also means that I wanted to be with men who were insiders because it was from men that I expected to get my own insider status.

Speaking of insider status, Christmas 1942, about a year after Pearl Harbor, I married Frank Hubbard, one of my college friends, a gentile from Westchester County whose American roots went back for generations. He had been drafted into the army. I was only eighteen and still an Austrian citizen. So this would be my part in the war: I became an American war bride. I stayed at Radcliffe, but lived on army posts with Frank on weekends and during the summer vacation until he was sent overseas. I will tell you a lot more about our relationship when I write about being a woman, marrying, and having children, but today I want to get on with sketching my life story.

In 1944, immediately after graduating from college, I took a job on a war project at Harvard, working with George Wald (my present husband) and another young, male scientist. I enjoyed the science, working in the lab, and being part of the war effort. I had become an American citizen, was married to an American GI, and felt at home in the United States. An insider.

After the war, Frank and I entered graduate school at Harvard and Radcliffe, he in English literature, I in biology. We lived a bohemian student life in a cold-water flat in a predominantly Black neighborhood of Cambridge among friends who lived like us. After a couple of years, Frank got bored with graduate school and apprenticed himself to a harpsichord maker in England. With mixed feelings, I interrupted my graduate work and went with him. He wanted to go to Europe. I wasn't sure I did. But soon I had a fellowship to work in a lab in London and began to like it. We

Ruth and Frank Hubbard, London, 1949

took a holiday in Paris. *Paris.* We passed through here on our way to the States ten years before. I loved Paris. Loved London. Europe felt like home. But not Vienna. I refused to go to Austria and, of course, Germany.

But I was also American. In 1948, I cast my first ballot, an absentee ballot from London and the only vote for president that I have ever felt good about, because I voted for Henry Wallace, candidate of the Progressive Party.

Frank and I bought a motorcycle and rode it through Holland, Belgium, Switzerland, Italy, France. Staying in youth hostels, barns, cheap hotels, and loving it all. The summer after we came back to the States, while Frank set up his workshop to build harpsichords, I went back to Europe. This time to a lab in Denmark.

Almost as soon as I arrived in Copenhagen, the Korean war began. In your first letter, you use that war as a reference point; it marked an insider/outsider axis in your life. It did for me as well. Being in Europe, able to read the European press, made it easy to be opposed to the war because it was so clear that the United States had wanted it to happen, was manipulating the United Nations to endorse the U.S. intervention, ignoring Nehru and anyone else who wanted to stop the fighting, provoking not only North Korea, but China as well. I came back to Cambridge that fall, 1950, completely opposed to the war and not expecting to find that everyone I knew supported it (everyone except my parents and brother, that is). Only one other person at the lab opposed the war, a fellow graduate student, from a family of pacifists. I was not a pacifist at the time, but at least he and I could talk without getting into a screaming fight. Soon Richard Nixon was suggesting we drop atom bombs on North Korea, go to war against China. Not since I first arrived in the United States had I felt like such a total outsider.

When I came back from Copenhagen, Frank and I decided to separate and although it was a mutual decision, it may have contributed to my sense of outsiderdom. But living alone and being "separated" was not as significant to my outsiderness as the war. So, once again, I began to look for insider spaces and joined pacifist or quasi-pacifist organizations, since they were the only groups I could find that opposed the war, groups like the

Committee for Nonviolent Action and the Central Committee for Conscientious Objectors. I also joined the Women's International League for Peace and Freedom, not a pacifist organization, but one opposed to the war. Coming closer to pacifist organizations made me rethink my opinion about World War II (my "good" war). I began to see the extent to which it had brutalized the world. And it had not "saved" European Jewry, which many people cited in its favor. Certainly those thoughts did not endear me to most of my friends and loosened more of my insider connections.

In 1953, while I was spending another year at a lab in Denmark, I traveled to Spain and Italy, then drove back to Copenhagen with friends. That meant driving through Germany. I had flown over Germany, gone through on trains. But drive, walk, eat, sleep in Germany? Speak German with Germans? We stopped as little as possible. The only sight-seeing was in Belsen, to look for a sign, tablet, memorial to the concentration camp. Not a word. To my surprise, I could not speak German. In Switzerland, I could manage, but in Germany, I understood but couldn't say a thing.

The same thing happened a few years later. I had recently married George and was expecting our baby. The International Biochemical Congress was meeting in Vienna and we decided to present papers. Again, I could not speak German, wouldn't tell anyone that this was where I was born. I felt European in Britain and France, Italy, Holland and Denmark. In Vienna, I was an American biochemist, traveling with my American husband, expecting our American baby.

In 1968, my parents decided to spend the summer in Austria, first Vienna, then Alt Aussee, a village on a lake not far from Salzburg, where we had spent our summers before we had to leave. I had loved Alt Aussee. That's where I learned to mow, stack hayricks, bring in the hay, speak the local dialect which my parents couldn't understand. Wore local dress—dirndls and clogs. My parents used to think it was a Nazi way to dress. I had liked it, loved the lake, meadows, mountains, and woods. I could well understand my father wanting to see it once more. He had been sick for many years and wasn't sure he'd be able to go if he put it off.

His heart began to fail almost as soon as the plane left Boston.

From then on the journey was punctuated by stays in hospitals. Finally he felt well enough so my parents could take the train from Vienna to Alt Aussee. Too ill to leave his hotel room, he could look at the lake from his window. A few nights later he died.

Gradually, over the next few years, I realized that I must go to Alt Aussee and Vienna, to connect with my past and come to terms with my father's death. He had his first heart attack right before I went to England in 1948 and I had thought that was when I stopped looking on him as my parent, became his parent instead. But whoever was parent to whom, I had underestimated the strength of our relationship. I had to go to where he died to come to terms with his death. But how? Alone? With family? Friends?

In April 1974, George and I were invited to attend a scientific meeting in Germany. Afterward, German friends drove us to Munich. What to do on a fine Sunday? Why not drive to Alt Aussee? It's not far. Our friends had never heard of the place and of course George didn't know it either. Why not go? After several sightseeing stops, we arrived.

I began to walk around, to look for the familiar places. It was exactly the way it had been thirty-seven years before. I wrote in my journal: "To see Alt Aussee is a dream come true, one I've dreamt often, but that has been tainted with the nightmare of irreplaceable loss. Yet here it is, completely unchanged—still a quiet village on a deep, dark lake, surrounded by mountains. The house where we used to live in as beautiful a spot as I remember, overlooking the village, in a meadow that rises to the woods. The lake a short walk away, along a footpath by a stream. It is beautiful and I can connect with the people and speak the language. What an enormous relief."

I couldn't stop walking, husband and friends in tow. Trying to live my way into a past that I had feared was lost or changed beyond recognition. Here it all was. Moving about I was keenly aware that this was where my father died, where he came to die.

Two days later, in Yugoslavia, I wrote:

I went to see my father
where he died.

When death came to your rescue
in the long and joyless
shadow of your life,
you met him in the place
you loved.

The midnight ring
by my bedside, the
long-distance voice of a stranger
speaking the strange tongue
I used to call my own;
mother telling me
your death,
rehearsing the yet unfamiliar words.
How often she has told them since.

I went to see my father
where he died.

Across a bright green meadow
full of yellow flowers, a father
runs with his child,
jumps into cold May water,
bubbling, playful.
Later in bed, he reads, she sleeps
guilty at the pleasure
of the unused intimacy.

I've photographed the house
in which you died, the lake,
the mountains, the house
in which we lived together.

I went to see you, father
where you died!
Let me show you my pictures
and be your child

in that bed
in that room
where you died and I
was a long-distance voice away!

      Long ago, the day death
      paid his morning call,
      kissed you lightly
      and promised to return,
      you asked me to go see
      your mother where she died.
      Asked in self-mourning
      and forgot.

      I went and saw the unmarked grave
      where, stranger in strange land,
      she died, too old and sick
      to know or care. You never

      asked me, so I never told.
      Did you not want
      to see your mother
      where she died?

They sent you home
by airmail, father,
when you died.
Put your ash
in an urn
in a box
on a shelf
in a vault
I never go to.

I went to see
where you were last alive!

I've seen the lake,
the house. I've
smelled the air!

That summer my daughter and I traveled to Europe. In
Amsterdam we suddenly decided to go to Alt Aussee "on the way to
Paris"—rather a roundabout way. Had I planned all along to
squeeze in these few days? I was keenly aware that at thirteen, my
daughter was the same age I was my last summer in Alt Aussee.
Now the two of us took long walks together, climbed mountains,
rowed on the lake. I wrote:

In the long ago time
that I only remember
in sleep
I used to walk these paths.

Now that I've walked them again,
my memories turn
from nightmares into dreams.

It was a healing I only half knew I needed. But I soon realized
that it didn't touch the pain and anger of my rejection by Vienna,
by Austria. I never saw the Nazis in Alt Aussee. My memories of it
were not filled with swastikas, the feeling that I was not wanted,
must get out. Alt Aussee disappeared like a loved one drowned at
sea, like my father leaving on a trip and not returning. To find it
again, unchanged, healed the forced break between past and
present. But now I needed to go to Vienna and make that connection, too. Relive the hurt and anger at being cast out. Go alone
without husband or child to cushion me against the past and
anchor me in the present.

So, in the spring of 1976 I flew to Vienna and moved into a
small pension in the part of the city where I lived in my earliest
years. I landed at midday and spent the afternoon walking. An
amazing experience (and not just because of jet lag). A mixture of
love, hate, admiration, rejection, and deep hurt. I started in the

Inner City and walked through the narrow streets with their sharp angles and corners. Then out to the Ring, the wide, tree-lined avenue that encircles it. When I lived in Vienna, I took pride in knowing all the streetcar routes, how to get from any point to any other. Here again, I mounted a streetcar, as in a dream, back to where I lived when the Nazis came, right by the canal that connects at both ends with the Danube. And that's where it grabbed me.

Until now I had almost been sight-seeing. Now I began to look in earnest. First the house where we lived when we left. Bombed out. Gone. I crossed the bridge over the canal to the quarter where we lived before that and where my grandparents and many other relatives lived, a bridge I used to cross almost every day. Each step I was inwardly screaming at the Nazis for forcing me out, killing those of us who couldn't get out. Crying, sobbing, furious. I walked past my grandmother's house. Gone. Past the temple two houses down. Of course, gone. In its stead a movie theatre and an empty lot. No sign, no tablet to suggest what was once there. Past my grammar school. Still there. Kids going home. A few shops still the same. The button and thread shop. The candy store. I entered and bought the kinds of candy I used to like: chocolate-covered bonbons with fruit centers and sugared fruit drops that taste like fruit. Then I walked into the Prater, Vienna's amusement park, past the ferris wheel of *Third Man* fame. On my way back, I briefly explored the area where my father's parents lived. Recognized their house and climbed the dim staircase to get a whiff of the musty, old-city smell. Then back into the street to study their windows. Of course, the temple near their house gone too. A grassy lot. No reminder of its history. Back in my pension, exhausted, I wrote:

I walk the streets of childhood
time a mix of then and now.
War ravaged, depleted of Jews,
this city more memory than present.
Gaping wounds of burned out synagogues.
Houses where I've lived gone.

War, battle scars, people's hate
have touched this place.
I must find my way
to the world that was
whose sights and sounds I remember.

I spent the next two weeks trying to feel my way back into the city where I had felt utterly at home and where I now knew all of four people. I strolled in neighborhoods and parks, went to theaters and museums, walked in the Vienna Woods, and ate in my parents' favorite coffee house. One sunny afternoon I took the tram to the outskirts, to one of the bridges over the Danube. People of all shapes and sizes were sunning themselves. In bathing suits or underpants and bras, poking their naked flesh at the sun.

The river boiled at my feet, going in all directions at once. Only in the middle could I see the current flowing to Bratislava, Budapest, Belgrade, the Black Sea, names familiar from geography class, places where I've never been. On my right a houseboat with a net hoisted high out of the water. I was surprised they fish in the Danube. Isn't it full of city pollution, mercury, lead? I sat down on the grassy embankment and wrote in my journal: "In every city I go to the river, looking for your dirty face. I am so glad to be sitting by your side, not having to imagine I am here. Bridges for trains, bridges for cars. Barges, ships. A man paddles a boat with one oar, nets hung over the side. In the distance, the hills of the Vienna Woods. I know their names, recognize the castles on top. Now they are restaurants, but at this range castles still. Vineyards climb the hills, neat strips of green and brown. The wine must be drunk sweet and fresh. It cannot be bottled. It doesn't keep!"

The trip made me feel more than ever that I'm European, not American. Although I didn't want to live in Vienna, I made my peace with it, accepted it as my former home. But in Vienna, too, I'm now an outsider. What was cannot be again. That means that there are places where I feel like an insider, such as my home in Cambridge, and here in Woods Hole where I spend almost half the year, writing, swimming, listening to the ocean, the wind, and the birds. And then there are corners in Europe, in London, the English Cambridge, Paris. And there is Alt Aussee. But not Vienna. It is an insider memory, an outsider now. My feelings of insiderness are grounded in family, friends and comrades, and in myself. My most insider space is with people.

It seems odd that I want to stop my "autobiography" at this point, some ten years ago. A lot has happened since. But in terms of insider/outsider, it fits better into some of the other topics I want to write you about. So, I'll stop for today.

Much love,

Ruth

Mothering gave something extraordinary to my life

Letter Five

Albuquerque, New Mexico
August 5, 1987

Dearest Ruth:

There's already so much in your first letters to which I want to respond! I love what's happening in this conversation. In your auto-biographical letter the description of being forced out of Vienna—being *cast out*, as you say—and then the return, years later, speak of a retrieval and coming to terms with memory so important, I believe, for us to really know who we are. Being ripped from one's home, especially as an adolescent, is hard. But how fortunate you are that you have been able to go back, make peace with that history, reclaim what you need from that.

I think, naturally, of the phenomenon of the past two decades in Latin America: the mass exiles, the disappearances of so many tens of thousands. Insider/outsider situations so complex and, often, tragic, it's hard to speak of them briefly in letters like these.

Something in your first letter, also takes me back to the struggles in Latin America. It's where you say " . . . I feel privileged to have arrived at a position where I don't have to integrate myself into work or political situations—become at least a quasi-insider—in order to survive." I don't think this is exactly what you had in mind, but when I hear "quasi-insider," I think of the Movement for National Liberation "Tupamaros" that was so strong in Uruguay in the seventies. People in the political opposition, who worked hard and patiently, for years, inside the system at all levels, as bank clerks, domestic help in embassies, medical personnel. They did this to be able to engage in political actions, extraordinary operations, involving entire towns, dramatic prison breaks (one in which one hundred and six prisoners escaped!), and successful political kidnappings that accomplished the retrieval of comrades being tortured and killed. These were only the most publicized results of this kind of long-term quasi-insiderness.

What proved, historically, a more profound by-product of that widespread collective sacrifice, was the fact that an entire population acquired a popular culture of struggle. So much so, that in 1980 when the dictatorship tried to ratify its existence through an electoral referendum in which the only square was one where the voter could mark "YES," more than 60% of those who went to the polls *wrote in* a "NO" that could not be ignored; it ultimately toppled the oppressive government.

So there you have, perhaps, another "category." People who carefully groom themselves in what we would have to call a quasi-insider position, waiting for their chance to do some small bit in an elaborate fabric of truly outsider action—in order to turn an outsider society around, make it more insider to people's needs.

Anyway, that's not really what I wanted to write about today. Having Sarah visiting here has me thinking of insider/outsider issues with regard to mothering.

I know that I grew up with pretty standard (if not traditional) expectations that I would eventually marry, have children, and form a family of my own.

My parents, as I've said, were not overly traditional in their attitudes. They thought about things, and they took risks others of their class, time, and culture generally didn't. I remember my early childhood as filled with adventure, especially after my parents moved us to New Mexico. We made weekend camping trips, summer voyages on freighters, were always searching for interesting experiences, and lively discussion filled our home. I have memories, like my dad reading the Father Brown* stories to us all after a picnic in the English countryside, that still evoke feelings of warmth and tenderness.

Sometimes I think my parents kept their family together primarily for the sake of their children. My father actually told me something like this once. I know he wasn't saying that this was the only reason. But it was a factor. As in most families of their generation and class, my parents put on what they saw as a harmonious face in public—you tried not to "wash your dirty laundry" out in the world; appearances were important. At home, for as long as I can remember, there has been a kind of continuous low-level bickering; as the years go by, it has sometimes become a visible part of my parents' public face. As my mother and father grow older I can also see the many ways in which they mean a great deal to one another, and how the life they have chosen has been the right one for them.

Family picture, right to left: Margaret, her father John, mother Elinor, brother Johnny, and sister Ann, Albuquerque, 1978. (Photo: Al Maddans)

* G. K. Chesterton's mystery series, featuring a Sherlock Holmes-type priest who always solved the crime.

So I grew up in an atmosphere in which family togetherness was valued—for the best reasons, as well as for some which may have been more questionable.

As a girlchild I assumed I too would find the right man, marry, and have children. From an early age I spoke of wanting three or four. I should also say that I had, in my parents, role models that were quite ahead of their time with regard to gender considerations. My father always did his share of work around the house, and still does. He was and is an exceptionally attentive parent. My mother had her own creative interests—first art, then translating—and these activities were important to her. She made them important. My father respected that. We all did.

I married young (eighteen) the first time, and remained with that husband for four years. It was a bad marriage, and we (luckily) had no children.

Then, as I've already mentioned, I went to New York, at some point decided to have a child on my own, and did. That was definitely an outsider act for the times. It was outsider, but I felt comfortable with it.

When my son was ten months old, we went to Mexico. There I soon married again, had my two oldest daughters, divorced after eight years, began living with someone else, and had my youngest. Ana's father and I also lived together for close to eight years.

In 1975, when Ana was six, Robert and I separated. After that I lived with another man, Antonio, for five years, and—eventually —with one more. But by the time Antonio and I had gone our separate ways, all but my youngest were not really children in the most dependent sense of that word.

In one way or another, to one degree or another, their lives had taken their own directions: Gregory was already living with the woman he would marry; and he was almost finished with his undergraduate degree. Sarah was close to finishing college as well.

Ximena had a year of high school left; she finished it and then came to live with Ana and me in Nicaragua.

When I decided to return to the United States, Ana was fourteen. I think my move affected her more than it did the others. You talk about how difficult it was for you to come to this country

80

from Austria at the same age, suddenly faced with a barrage of cultural differences at a time when you were struggling to discover who you were and would be. Ana suffered this acutely. She literally learned English in six months, and did very well at "adjusting" to a whole different lifestyle. But inside, I know she is still dealing with the change.

What I would like to explore here are the ways I have been insider or outsider as a mother, when insider and when outsider, and how that has affected my children—either positively or adversely. I'd also like to look at how my insider/outsiderness has affected each one of my children, at least inasmuch as I've been able to know how he or she feels about it.

I spoke about my parents having stayed together in part for their children. That was an insider act, vis-à-vis their class and culture. It was something I never did. It occurred to me only initially—and under great pressure from him—to remain with Sergio because we had children. I remember his threats, that I "would never find anyone willing to accept a woman with three kids(!)," and I remember how that hurt . . . for a time. But I rather quickly crawled out from under that intimidation, left him anyway, and (just as quickly) linked my children's and my lives to the man who happily was a father to the three existing children as well as to one more whom he and I engendered.

From about that time on, I became someone who readily understood that her basic drive was towards self-realization—not on an individual plane only, but very much including what I felt I needed to do creatively and politically.

I ended relationships with relatively little fanfare when I saw that remaining in them was holding me back. In this way of being, I became the central pillar in my children's sense of family; an insider to them in terms of holding the family together, an outsider, perhaps, in that as a mother I was hardly similar to other mothers with whom they were familiar.

Indeed I became a rather unconventional (outsider) mother to my kids in many ways. I never saw mothering as something one did full-time. It didn't even occur to me. I always knew I would write, work, earn my own way, travel, take on projects that demanded as much if not more time than mothering did. When I separated from the fathers of my children I felt they (the fathers) should help with the children's economic support. None of them really did, or they did so sporadically and never enough. This created problems. It pushed me into an outsider position relative to my class and culture, but into an insider position vis-à-vis the vast majority of the world's mothers.

I loved my children and wanted to be with them. I tried to learn how *really* to be with them when that was possible. But I always made use of alternative care—the Dalton School's program for unwed mothers and Jewish Philanthropies, in New York City; household help in Mexico; live-in school programs in Cuba.

From before Gregory's birth, I knew that the most precious gift I could give my children would be an open door to their own independence. I actively wanted to make them independent. I remember with Gregory doing things like refusing to boil the formula during his first few months, consciously choosing for him what I believed would be a healthy acquaintance with germs (and therefore antibodies) as opposed to depending on sterilization. I dressed him lightly even in winter. I toted him around on the subway; I wanted him to be able to adapt to any bed, any environment, any contingency.

Gradually, I sought more profound ways to develop independence in my kids. I encouraged them to set their own limits, make their own decisions, select and pack their own clothing for travel, explore, learn.

When Gregory one summer, at the age of ten, announced he would be taking an interprovincial bus to the Cuban city of Pinar del Rio, I was delighted. I watched him pack an astronomy book and a couple of changes of socks, then drove him to the bus station. I didn't really think he'd go off for several days as he said he would, but when he didn't come home the following morning but called instead from his destination, I knew I'd been wrong. Neighbors—especially the mothers among them—were aghast. As a mother, they definitely considered me an outsider. But I knew then and know now that this was one of the healthiest things I ever encouraged my child to do.

It was the same with my daughters, although from a social point of view much harder—this kind of an attitude was (maybe) okay with boys; it was unheard of with girls. Ana has recently taken me to task for failing to accompany her on routine doctor's visits in Havana. She clearly feels that this was a loss, leaving her insecure and needful today. So at least some of what I then felt was making my children more independent is perceived by them as having been more detrimental than strengthening.

Granted, raising the children in Cuba provided a physical context where all this was much easier; the streets were safe, there was no drug scene, young people could be left to their own devices with much more peace of mind than in the United States. On the other hand, some of my feminist ideas struck an unresponsive echo in Havana—although equality was written into the new revolutionary way of life, Latin American traditionalism with regard to male and female roles was still entrenched in many areas.

Where I expected my son to wash and iron his clothes, help with the housework, learn to cook, his contemporaries often were not placed under the same demands. Where I encouraged my daughters to *resist* offering these services to their male counterparts, they did not always have the company of their peers. In other words, in the home I created—sometimes in spite of the men with whom I lived, sometimes with their cooperation—I worked to preserve my own creative time, I worked to help my children become independent, and I tried to respect each of them as an individual.

I was not a mother who sponsored Girl Scout troops (or their Cuban equivalent). I wasn't much given to taking my kids, with their friends, to an outing at the zoo. I often used my particular skills (writing, artwork, later photography) to invent things that delighted a classroom or another of my children's peer groups. I tried to set examples of intellectual and cultural curiosity, creativity, adventure, risk-taking, truthfulness, defense of justice, thoughtfulness, consideration towards others, historical perspective, tolerance without betraying one's principles, and a loyalty to causes and people that deserve one's love.

In general, I think my kids have grown up healthy and vibrant, inquisitive, sensitive, loving, inventive, creative, whole. All but one have always been fiercely independent. And that one has become more so in recent years.

Although each of my children at different times has resented certain aspects of the ways in which they were raised—one feels he would have preferred not to have been away at school, all would undoubtedly have preferred less change in terms of my relation-ships with their fathers and/or the men with whom I've lived, three have taken me to task for not spending more time with them—I think they have increasingly come to feel they had a fairly solid and positive family life.

I think the single factor in my own life which has most affected my children's ongoing condition as insiders and/or outsiders, is the fact that I have moved with them—not only from country to country, but from political system to political system, and in Ana's case even from one culture and language to another culture and language radically different from those in which she grew up.

If I have trouble, sometimes, understanding how my roots and experiences come together to produce a life, my children have the same problem—intensified by the fact that they did not choose to go here or there; they were taken.

My son has often spoken of how his U.S. birthright, his early years in Mexico, and his coming of age in Cuba, combine to inform an identity he cannot yet fully define.

Sarah has chosen to remain in Cuba; she currently works there as a chemical engineer. Her isolation from this country is hard on both of us. She considers moving to Mexico, and spent several months last year accrediting herself as an engineer in that country. But, as she told me on this visit, as someone who has grown up almost entirely in a socialist society, she's not really sure she could adapt to Mexico.

Ximena lives in Mexico but seems somewhat ambivalent towards it. Both Sarah and she, as Mexican citizens, are limited insofar as their possibilities for living closer to me are concerned.

Ana, now living in New York, has more frequently than any of the others expressed a real anguish about her sense of rootlessness; she was born in Mexico, grew up in Cuba and Nicaragua, and has come to the United States and become a citizen. She feels a certain marginality, at this point, in all of these cultures.

So, although I am sure I gave my kids an exciting life, based on worthy principles, and encouraged them to develop a sense of self-worth and independence, I also know that the nature of my journey denied them the solidity of stable roots that might have given them a sense of insiderness as regards a particular national origin.

Mothering gave something extraordinary to my life. Being a mother, with each of my four children, is precious on so many levels. Now I'm excited about becoming a grandmother: Gregory and Laura are expecting a child in October; Ximena and Fito in February.

Family picture, left to right: Ximena, Ana, Gregory, Margaret, Sarah, Albuquerque, 1986. (Photo: Jack Levine)

I was something of an outsider mother, yet I felt very inside in so being. My children, in the light of my particular mothering, seem to feel inside in terms of their communication with me (solidly so in the cases of Gregory and Sarah; adequately so insofar as Ximena and Ana are concerned—though I think there's still a

85

way to move with both of them). But they have frequently felt outside in terms of their family being "different," the variety of countries in which we've lived, the ways in which they have had to fend for themselves.

As we get older, we talk about these things. Sometimes in recriminating ways. More often just because we're naturally given to analyzing our lives, and try—each of us—to learn from how they have evolved.

I don't think I honestly ever gave up anything either to have children or to care for them. Everything I've wanted to do, I somehow found a way of doing—children or not. In that sense I was outsider to the typical housewifely role; but insider to my own needs and realization.

I do not, of course, believe that procreation is woman's primary role, nor that women "realize" ourselves by having children. I deeply resent the socialization that makes many women feel incomplete without children, and I believe men need to learn to share a great deal more in childraising—all the endless drivel about their "helping" has long ago left me cold. In spite of these beliefs, mothering my own children has been and continues to be an important part of my life.

In 1975 I wrote a poem called "Motherhood" which might more accurately have been titled "Womanhood," for it contained most of what I was then able to say about the female condition. Or at least my own womanness. I have since pondered that poem's title, and wondered what in fact it did say about being a woman and being a mother, the overlaps and/or separateness of both conditions and the implicit insider/outsider contradictions.

Anyway, these are just some thoughts about mothering. Initial thoughts, probably.

So much love,

Margaret

By remembering I become more
a member in my life.

Letter Six

Woods Hole, Massachusetts
August 7th, 1987

Dearest Margaret:

Today I want to write you about what it means to me to be human, a female human, a woman. One reason I am enjoying this correspondence so much is that I have come to realize that by remembering, I become more of a member in my life and many of those I remember join in that membership with me. So, apart from my life being a quilt made of patches of inside and outside in all sorts of unexpected conjunctions and combinations, these re-memories give me fresh glimpses and insights and open up inside spaces that I didn't expect to find. Maybe that's why old people dwell on memories. As we grow old, we lose friends and connections and our insiderness comes to lie more and more in our remembered memories. Young people can afford to forget their memories because they are busy forging their inside lives as they move forward.

A good place to start is right here in Woods Hole, because this is where I feel most insider, like you in your foothills in Albuquerque. In a way, Woods Hole means to me now what Alt

87

Aussee meant to me as a child. It's where I can go barefoot, wear whatever I want, or nothing at all in my own backyard. Thinking about it earlier today, I realized that this is where I feel most inside nature and myself. It is not raw nature, wilderness; it has streets and houses and all the vegetation has been planted, but it's as close to nature as I can live for extended periods of time. I can travel to jungles, deserts, or rugged mountains, but I'm not likely to live there for long.

When I was in Vermont that amazing, strange summer before college, I used to lie on the ground, look up at the sky, and get a wonderful, adolescent sense of oneness with nature. It is a feeling I often try to recapture, my most insider feeling, when nature feels like home. And I get it here where I can see the ocean change, the tides cycle, the beach be different after each high tide. When I'm in Woods Hole, I always know the phase of the moon and when it will rise and set, even when the clouds are too dense for me to see it.

I plant a ridiculously small vegetable garden and watch things grow and ripen. And this summer I have watched a family of wood-chucks, that has dug its hole among the raspberry bushes right by the house, get at each kind of vegetable when it's just about ready to pick and always beat me out. They ate all the different lettuces I planted and the basil. The tomatoes began to be to their liking just about the time I thought of picking them. I still seem to like mint better than they do, but they are getting to like it, too. The other day, they ate a perennial poppy right down to the ground. Then there is the rather tame robin who comes for his worms, the occasional wasps' nest. Late in the spring a very large snapping turtle laid eggs near the pond on the way to the beach. We thought they'd never make it. Then the other day a string of tiny turtles marched down to the pond in single file. So, though it's not wild, it is not city either, and it is where I feel most insider. And also most at one with my body because I can go to the beach as soon as I wake every morning, stretch, meditate, and take a long swim in my bare skin, with nothing but birds and fish around. That's my real meditation, when I find my rhythm of breathing and movement in the water. After that, I'm ready for breakfast, work, what the day brings.

As for people, I need my family, although I like it a lot when I am here alone. I also have friends among the year-round inhabitants—the carpenter, the plumber, a potter, a musician who sands and cleans floors for a living. Rather gentle folk, quite different from my Harvard colleagues. Mostly I enjoy the privilege of being able to write, read, bicycle, swim, while feeling that I am part of my natural surroundings.

It's a privilege because the way most of us live, it is very difficult to feel at one with oneself, and especially so for a woman.Our society, the outside, imposes such a lot of disabling standards that make it difficult for us to feel insiders, even in our own bodies. It can define what it means to be a woman, something I want to be. It can get inside our heads through advertising, television dramas, literature, art. Since I am not like that—none of us is—I become an outsider not only to "woman" but to myself (since I know I am a woman). Women have to spend an inordinate amount of energy trying to feel at home in our own bodies as well as bringing those of us who do not fit the prescribed standards into our inside world. That's why I think we have to begin by doing whatever it takes to feel unalienated, like insiders, in our own bodies and with our friends and comrades in the groups with which we identify. It takes communal work to get to feel whole because of the many insidious messages we get about products, services and so-called health care that are supposed to improve us, make us feel better, look better, be better.

This dialogue for instance

It takes group work to sort out the mystifications and lies and get beyond them. I try to do some of that with my students and when I give talks, but it takes more sharing than usually happens in those settings. Some of it I can do by myself and that's where my morning stretching, meditating, and swimming comes in. But much of it is better done with others.

I have been trying to think about when and how I learned to listen to my body. Surely not as a child because my parents, being doctors, were full of prescriptions that had little to do with how I felt. I am sure they, like most of their contemporaries, believed that a child cannot possibly know what's good for her or him. There were rules about bedtime, food, clothes, cleanliness, weight, exercise, fresh air, you name it. None of these encouraged me to develop the habit of listening inside.

What did help was that because I was rather clumsy and not well coordinated when I started school, my parents enrolled me in a gymnastics and acrobatics class given by the fiancée of one of my grown-up cousins. I quickly learned to move the way I wanted, which put me not only more in touch with myself, but made me a

Ruth near Vienna, 1930.

better athlete in school and therefore more of an insider socially.

But I don't think I began to feel at one with my body and listen to it until briefly during my two pregnancies around 1960 and then in earnest when I encountered yoga some ten years later. I was introduced to yoga by a friend who was a birth coach and later became a midwife. She had the perfect voice and manner to teach yoga and it clicked for me from the first breath. I have since then gone to classes that felt all wrong and to others that were wonderful, and have come to realize that with yoga, like everything else, there is no single "right" way that works for everyone.

When I talk with friends who have struggled with addictions to alcohol or cigarettes or with eating disorders, I always feel that the answer is to get to be an insider in your body, respond to the signals it gives about what will make it feel right. Am I being naive? Is that precisely what is difficult to do? But how else avoid the gimmicks that people keep pushing at you?

The place where I have to deal with this most directly right now are the signs of getting old, whatever that means. If I want to continue to be an insider to myself, I have to accept that my skin, hair, body are aging. I don't really know what "old" means. When I was twenty, fifty seemed old, my present age positively decrepit. But that's the point. Our youth-oriented, consumerist culture tries to sell body-changing pills, potions, operations, devices to all of us, no matter what age we are, and makes all of us outsiders to what we see when we look in the mirror first thing in the morning, before we have "fixed" ourselves. But it especially makes old people outsiders, and of course old women more than men, because old men can look distinguished and craggy. Old women are presented as ugly, frightening, repulsive—witches. Especially when our vision, hearing, or mobility decreases, we are treated like incompetents, children, which means outsiders to who we know we are.

As a professor I am used to meeting a measure of respect from the people I come in contact with at work and in my neighborhood, where people know me. But when I step beyond those limits I often find that I am not expected to understand what people are trying to tell me, am expected to be a nuisance and in the way. This attitude is even more obvious toward my mother, who is in her nineties and hard of hearing. People infantilize her, ask how old she is and say things like "God bless her" (third person). They talk to me about her rather than addressing her, even before they know that she doesn't hear well.

A few years ago, when the Boston Women's Healthbook Collective was getting *The New Our Bodies, Ourselves* together, they invited a number of women between roughly fifty-five and seventy-five to talk about what it's like to get old and be old. They didn't know whether we'd come and what would happen. We started to meet hesitantly at first, but soon we met regularly every two or three weeks for the better part of a year and loved it. It was exciting to be in a group of older feminists. Usually, if I am with feminists, they are younger than I and if I am with women my age or older, they aren't feminists, or at least don't think of themselves that way.

These women, about ten of us, had lived varied lives. Most of us—I think all of us—had been married or were married. Several were widows, one or two were divorced. All had spent a large part of our lives taking care of people—husbands, children, parents—and all had woken up at some point and realized that we are people too. And not just people, but women, who have needs and rights, especially the right occasionally to ask other people to take care of us. We had lived quite different kinds of lives and that made it all the more interesting. Most of the women were not very political, in the sense of being active in political movements, but we didn't have major political disagreements and it was a very productive and exciting experience for all of us. I think the main thing for me was the quality of insiderness, all of us very different, but also with similar assumptions and very open to each other.

That brings me to something else I have been thinking about and wanting to explore with you and that is my sense of vulnerability in the women's movement. Just this morning, I had a conversation with a friend in which I was saying angry things about Catherine McKinnon and Andrea Dworkin and some of the women who support them on pornography and who are now congealing into a similarly rigid position about prenatal and other reproductive technologies, like in vitro fertilization and "surrogate" motherhood. Of course, I am opposed to all or much of this, like they are, and in fact was one of the first people to talk about the destructive implications of these technologies for women. But I don't want a whole bunch of new laws passed that tell women what we mustn't do. So, I want to educate, publicize, agitate, warn, but not put more power into the hands of the state. As with pornography, these women want to outlaw all these things and, what infuriates me even more, define themselves as the only true opponents of these technologies and us as supporters of the technologies, compromisers, "liberals."

However, the question I'm asking myself now is why they infuriate me so. And I think it is that I am open to disagreements, discussions, debates, but I don't want to be read out of certain groups within the women's movement. When that happens, the word in my head is "fascists!" And I immediately revert into the hurt of being made an outsider (outcast) in Vienna, where I had felt totally inside and safe.

Thinking about these things since we began this exploration together, I have realized that I probably did not let down my guard within political groups until I began to identify as a feminist and a member of the women's liberation movement. "Scientist" is a group identity, too, and I feel part of it, but there always was too much sexual and professional politics for me to let down my guard and feel truly inside. But since my Viennese school was a girls' school—all schools were segregated by sex—joining women, identifying as a woman to work with other women, has allowed me to feel inside in a way that resembles that earlier, childish-confident way. And I think this is why I get so angry (frightened?) when I feel my insiderness in the women's movement threatened, not by disagreement, but by a kind of rigidity that permits only one way to look at complex issues like childbearing or sexuality. Rightly or wrongly, I immediately call that fascist and respond very negatively. And while I accuse them of generating insider/outsider divisions within the movement, I am emotionally unable to build the bridges we would need in order to heal that split.

I would love to know whether you have learned to deal with insider/outsider splits among erstwhile comrades and allies and how you do it.

Much love,

Ruth

Only The hope That They will be strong, independent, decent, responsible people.

Letter Seven

Woods Hole, Massachusetts
August 10th, 1987

Dear Margaret:

I've been scribbling notes to myself all morning about the letter I want to write you in response to yours of August 5th about marriage and motherhood, which have been a braid of insider and outsider experiences for me.

Like most little girls, I grew up expecting that some day I would marry and have children. But in Vienna that did not exclude having a profession and expecting to earn my living. Early in the century, the universities had opened their doors to women, economic pressures encouraged two-earner families, and the class structure assured a pool of household and childcare workers who enabled middle-class women to pursue professional or business careers. All my mother's women friends were physicians, musicians, or teachers and all of them practiced their professions whether or not they were married or had children. In our circles, no women stayed home. After I came to the States, I was such an outsider that the feminine mystique Betty Friedan has written about never penetrated my consciousness.

I entered college intending to go to medical school, a highly unoriginal choice for the daughter of physicians. Marrying Frank Hubbard half-way through college did not change that. As I've told you before, my marrying Frank was an attempt to shake off my outsiderness by becoming at once a wife (= grown-up) and part of an American family. I married Westchester County and Thanksgiving and Christmas celebrations as much as Frank. I am not suggesting that I exploited him. We were both very young and had mixed agendas. Frank, in his turn, needed me as a shield against an over-ambitious mother, who was loading hopes she had nurtured for many more children onto the only one she was, to her great sorrow, able to have. Her husband was a commercial artist and not easy to squeeze into a proper Westchester mold. Her son, after many struggles with which I helped quite a bit, managed to parlay his outsider approach to life into starting the modern harpsichord revival in the United States. The poor lady would buy me clothes I would not wear and suggest hair styles I did not accept and occasionally ask whether it wasn't about time for my husband to begin to support me so I could have children. But that wasn't on our minds.

Because my interests changed, I became a biologist and not a physician, but during the eight years Frank and I lived together, I always earned more money than he did and had we not separated, this would have continued for quite a while without either of us minding. Obviously, trying to become a harpsichord maker was more problematic than becoming a scientist. As for children, neither of us felt ready. The two times I thought I might be pregnant, we agreed I'd have an abortion despite the difficulties it would have involved in those days. Fortunately, it wasn't necessary.

Frank and I separated as friends in 1950, but didn't bother to get a divorce until two years later, when I went to Copenhagen and it seemed more practical not to be formally connected. So, neither our marriage nor our separation were traditional. Marriage was an insider step that served our needs at the moment, but we used the format to construct a largely outsider life in which Frank took on a major share of the household, such as it was, and I provided most of the income—not the standard 1940s model. Our separation was a great relief. We had not been wildly unhappy, but we no longer wanted to live together. This was also my first experience of living alone since I had gone directly from living with my parents to being married. But while I enjoyed living alone, I felt that it was an asocial, outsider, way to be. In Cambridge and later in Copenhagen, all my closest friends were married and had children and I looked on that as the right (insider) way to live.

By then I acknowledged that I was in love with George and he with me, but he was married to someone else and had two children. To break up that family contradicted our beliefs about how to live one's life. So we kept trying to stop our relationship, though at best in halfhearted ways. To make an all-too-long story short, we tried to fool ourselves and each other about this for many years until George finally left his marriage and we started to live together. But he didn't in fact get a divorce for several more years. In effect, we kept our relationship in the closet for well over a decade, a thoroughly outsider experience that meant that I lived a very important part of my life as a secret from my associates at work and from all but my closest friends and family.

When George and I finally married, we took it for granted that we'd have children if we could. I don't think we bothered to talk much about it. It was just the way it was—for both of us. And indeed Elijah was born shortly after we married and Debbie two years later.

Being married to George, a well-known scientist and Harvard professor and someone I loved very much, and having two children with him (a boy and a girl in that order, yet!) clearly were very insider experiences. But since I had no intention of stopping my work, I had to come up with all sorts of individual solutions to deal with the reality that our society considers this an outsider way to live and makes no provisions (then even less than now) to enable women and men to work outside the home and have children. More than that, by trying to combine my career and family without a feminist consciousness (and at that point I had none), I—the nouveau-super-insider—developed outsider identities in both my work and family situations. I could no longer participate in my work as fully as I had done before, could not attend as many seminars and out-of-town meetings as I had been used to. My work, which until then had spread into evenings and weekends whenever necessary, now had to be scheduled nine-to-five, when my helper was available. And not only did I have to do it, I wanted to, because I wanted to be with my children. I was not a full-time mother, either. I rarely took my children to the playground and had little time to be with other mothers. I felt overworked and lonely, too deeply embroiled in the world of men, yet coming to feel an outsider in it; not deeply enough into the world of women, an outsider there as well.

Ruth, George, Elijah, Debbie (and Brian), Woods Hole, 1969. (Photo: T. Polumbaum)

This was a surprise because although I never felt it would be a disaster if we didn't have children, I did feel I was an outsider by not having them and expected being married and a mother to constitute automatic insiderness. (Some years ago, when George and I were in West Africa, I was struck by the fact that people—children, but also adults—in the villages would start up conversations with us not with "do you have children?" but "how many children do you have?" completely taking it for granted that we had them.) It is in that sense that I had previously felt an outsider—living alone, a woman scientist, and worse yet, a woman who had an illicit lover. So, when I did have children, I saw it as an insider thing, something that made me part of society. In addition, I felt that the process of pregnancy and birth made me an insider with womankind back into prehistory.

97

Living in overmedicalized Boston in the late 1950s, that meant I had to do major research to find an obstetrician who would promise to let me be awake during labor and birth, since the standard procedure involved a form of anaesthesia called twilight sleep, and induction of the birth. The woman would wake up hours later and drowsily ask a nurse (of course, a total stranger) whether she'd had a baby, was it okay, a girl or boy, etc. Adrienne Rich had her children in Boston at about that time and has written it all out.* Having a Ph.D., being a biologist, having parents inside the Boston medical system, I managed to locate a youngish obstetrician who interfered minimally for those days, promised to let me be awake unless there was an emergency, reassured me that thirty-five was not old for a first pregnancy (it is considered that now!), and urged me to go ahead and live my life as I had been doing—work, exercise, whatever. He also advised me to have "rooming-in," an elitist extra, which would let me keep my baby in my room starting forty-eight hours after birth, and promised that the baby would be brought to me regularly for feedings from the time it was born and not given milk or sugar water in the nursery. All kinds of wonderful privileges! To me this was part of being an insider with womanhood and nature, although it meant being an outsider to the experience of most of the women I knew.

You said the other day, that you, too, insisted on being awake for Gregory's birth. I wonder why it is that although our insider/outsider configurations were so different, both of us were adamant that to have a baby meant to be awake during the birth.

Elijah's birth was a spectacular experience! I remember thinking as I was pushing him out that nothing, but nothing, I had done until then—work, publications, travel, anything else—equaled the excitement and sense of accomplishment of giving birth to this tiny, perfect person. And of course he was terrific, wide awake, wonderfully calm, looking all around him. The nurses, who were not used to awake mothers and unanaesthetized babies, were flabbergasted that that's how a newborn baby could be. (Isn't that frightening?) And again this was insider to me, but outsider in my immediate surroundings.

I got overly involved with Elijah when he was an infant. I took

* *Of Woman Born* by Adrienne Rich. New York: W. W. Norton, 1976.

six months off from work and went nuts staying home with a small baby. I guess, for once, I was an insider in my culture, but I was an outsider to myself and my needs. Of course, I enjoyed playing with him and nursing him, in fact I ended up nursing him for eleven months, long after I went back to work, another outsider thing for that time; but staying home for six months was too much.

When I went back to work, a Black woman who had raised many children took care of Elijah weekdays. She taught me more than all the "experts" and books. She was big on treating children like people in their own right, refused to use a leash or harness to tie Elijah into his carriage or stroller (leashes are for dogs, harnesses for horses, she told me), or to have gates at the top or bottom of our stairs. She assured me she would help him find out what he could safely do and how to get up and down stairs when he was ready. As a result, Elijah used to scare the daylights out of unsuspecting visitors by cautiously slithering downstairs on his tummy once he began to crawl. So, like you, I was an insider to my ideas of what it means to be a free-spirited, independent human being, but outsider to many of the accepted rules.

When Debbie was born, two years after Elijah, my nine-to-five helper stayed with me even though I took five months' leave from work. That was great because it gave me a chance to have time for myself and also be with my children. But it was a matter of course that I would go back to full-time work after that. To my surprise, attitudes had begun to change in those two years. More women were working outside the home and it felt like less of an outsider thing to be doing.

In retrospect I realize that the price I paid for being a professional and a mother, who wanted a lot of time with her children, was that I put my political activities on hold. I wrote checks, but did not get personally involved, not even in the civil rights movement. I listened to the Selma march on the radio as well as to the U.S. invasion of Cuba and the "Cuban missile crisis." My politics didn't change, but I did not take an active part in the support and protest movements. During this period my brother was politically very active as a lawyer in San Francisco and became my connection to political activism as well as to the Beat movement. Only in the mid-sixties, when my children were older and the

Vietnam war and the women's liberation movement heated up, did I become actively involved and begin to march, speak, and write about political issues.

George and I started taking Elijah and Debbie to rallies and demonstrations from the time they were little. Elijah enjoyed them and even as a small boy considered himself part of the movement, wearing political buttons and writing and talking about politics in the early grades in school. Debbie had too lively an imagination. The sight of police, especially in full riot gear, with helmets, nightsticks, and dogs, terrified her so that she could not conjure up a sense of identification (or insiderness) with the people with whom she was demonstrating.

Getting both children to be their own people was very much what I saw mothering to be about. But I also made choices for them, like sending them to private schools through 8th grade. That was an insider thing to do in our social milieu in Cambridge, but an outsider thing vis-à-vis our politics. I had been so bored in public high school in Brookline and felt that the solidity of my elementary education in Vienna had stood me in such good stead that I wanted my kids to learn the basics of reading and writing and math, and enjoy them, and then do what they wanted with it. I've talked with Debbie about that recently and she agrees that having had a good early education has made things much easier for her. So, I am conflicted about how appropriate that was.

Elijah responded to the contradiction by developing a special persona between the ages of about eight and twelve. He had long hair (everyone mistook him for a girl and he'd quietly say "I'm a boy" and be unruffled by the "mistake" or the fluster that followed the correction); wore deeply colored woven shirts from Oaxaca, of which he acquired a sufficient number so he never needed to wear anything else; of course, narrow leg jeans; and innumerable political buttons on his chest—anti-war, Black Panther, etc. He was a small boy until after adolescence and you could hardly see his chest for all the buttons. Of course he played the guitar (a small guitar his half-brother, David, had bought him) and sang. And that was Elijah, totally different from his friends and apparently feeling fine about it. I am still grateful to his 6th grade teacher, a quite conservative man. At a time when I felt that one wrong move and we'd have a twelve-year-old druggy drop-out on our hands (Cambridge was not like Havana in this regard!), he stimulated Elijah to write and speak in class about the various political causes whose buttons he wore on his chest and to research different kinds of drugs and their range of effects. And Elijah continued to feel sufficiently comfortable, supported, and accepted in his outsider persona, that he didn't join a cult or get into drugs.

Something interesting happened instead. When Elijah had been in private school through 8th grade (so eight years of school plus four years of preschool), he announced that he was not going to a private high school or prep school, which is where just about all his classmates were heading. He would go to the public high school in Cambridge or to a small alternative public high school that had opened a few years earlier, called Pilot School. Students were admitted to Pilot by a lottery weighted so as to represent all the different areas and ethnic and racial groups in Cambridge. At the point at which Elijah was admitted, he exclaimed "I'm off the track!" Despite his outsider persona, he had felt confined by a sense of limited, narrow insiderness, where everyone knew the next step—from the right nursery school to the right kindergarten, private school, prep school, Harvard (or Yale), medical (or law) school, etc. Debbie was not so sure she wanted to get "off the track" but also ended up deciding to go to Pilot School. Now, many years later, both feel they made the right choice because by going to public school they (and we, their parents) became part of Cambridge in a way none of us had while they were in private schools. Since high school, Elijah and Debbie have stayed close to us and have often lived at home, but as separate people with their own lives.

So, what does that say about the meanings of mothering for me? I did not see it as part of my identity, my insiderness to myself. I saw it as a way to feel more inside in the larger society, but did not feel that that meant I had to do it the "right" way. I did not feel it was my responsibility to turn my children into certain kinds of people, except in the sense you have said of being honest, integrated in themselves, conscious of the world around them, responsible, etc. I think I have succeeded to different degrees and in different ways with the two of them. Their approaches to life and the lives they are choosing to live are different, but neither is overly bound by conventions and they are able to find or construct environments in which they can be insiders, while being outsiders towards many standard expectations. They have also learned to use their outsiderness to energize them, Debbie in her earlier work with incarcerated women and now, as a lawyer, with refugees, and Elijah in living and feeling at home in far-away places, making music, learning what languages he needs, and living in whatever way the people live where he happens to be. My comfort in my own outsiderness has made it unproblematic for me to let my children construct their own outsider realms. And I have been able to do it without getting freaked out that they are "different," like many parents do, in Cambridge academia as much as in middle America. I see them as their own people and do not feel that I have failed when they do not conform to the world's expectations. I have never had very concrete expectations for them. Only the hope that they will be strong, independent, decent, responsible people, who feel comfortable in their own skins and accept other people as they are.

Mind you, that's easy to say now. I have often asked myself how I would have felt if they had gotten heavily into drugs, were heavy smokers or alcoholics, or on the other hand, totally conformist. What if Debbie had become wildly "feminine," with fancy clothes, lots of make-up, and a world that revolved around pleasing men? What if they had gone real straight, become business executives, corporation lawyers, aspiring members of the scientific or medical establishment? Obviously I would try to keep our relationship going, but it would be more difficult. So, I set great store by outsiderness in this society—for them and for me—and am prepared to give my children whatever leeway and support they need to construct satisfying lives in their outsiderland.

As for me, my family is an important part of my insider world. Yet, I often don't feel supported by George or Elijah. What I have come to realize in writing you about this is that much of the insider relationship, especially with George, has to do with the long, continuous history we share. I share many parts of my life more with women friends than with George, but we have known each other longer and more continuously and closely, than anyone else.

George and I met forty-four years ago, when I was twenty (and he thirty-seven) and have been lovers (with a few minor interruptions) for forty-three of them (and I am now sixty-three!). That's what makes us insiders to each other. Things at times may be lacking in our relationship, but its on-going reality is profound and feels very moving. George is old, nearly eighty-one, and we have shared the longest part of our lives. That's why we are insiders with each other.

Before I finish, I want to come back to something you said on the phone the other day when you told me that you now know that Gregory's and Laura's child will be a girl and that they and you feel ambivalent about knowing that before she is born, but that it is almost inevitable because of the repeated "echograms" (ultrasound scans) Laura has been given in Paris. Because of the focus of my recent work about the medicalization of pregnancy and birth and the new pregnancy interventions that are supposed to make it all so much safer, these kinds of issues have been at the center of my concerns. And they are insider/outsider questions in a quite literal sense: it has become intolerable to the medical profession to have the inside of women's wombs remain opaque. One way of getting control of women's reproductive capacities has been to insist on looking in and to make it seem unsafe *not* to look in, to bring what is inside, out into the open. Unfortunately, the reality is that they still cannot be sure that ultrasound scans are safe and periodically there is a conference that comes up with recommendations to minimize their use unless there is a good reason. Meanwhile, medical practitioners have lost the skills folks used to have in your days as a midwife that let you keep track of what goes on inside *from outside*, by feeling a woman's distended belly and putting your ear or a stethoscope up against it. Instead, they now put her under a machine and the practitioner and her partner, if she has one, look *away from her*, at a screen, to *see* the fetus, watch it move, etc. It's no longer going on inside her; it's happening out there, on the screen. One doesn't have to feel, and listen to, *her* body to find out. She is no longer the person in whom the fetus moves. She is the barrier that makes it difficult to see the fetus and examine it properly, a barrier that must be made transparent.

(I don't want to worry you about the possible dangers of ultrasound. So far no problems have been noticed, but there is no question that at higher intensities ultrasound disrupts cells. The question is: does it do no harm at the intensities that are used clinically? It took some twenty years to get evidence that X-rays are bad for fetuses. Now, despite the fact that there hasn't been that long a time to monitor the effects of ultrasound, it is used widely and its use is not at all restricted to the rare situations where it seems clearly justified. It's now pretty much routine. Of course, women, or couples, can refuse, but most people don't know that and, what's more, how do you have the guts to refuse a doctor the use of something that he or she tells you will make the pregnancy and birth safer for your baby? I even allowed the obstetrician to take a series of X-rays just before Elijah was born, because he said he had to know whether the baby was pointing head down or breech and couldn't be sure by feeling. And I was damned sure it was risky even though all the data weren't in at the time.)

Women have that mysterious space inside us that make men feel outsiders. For a long time physicians have tried to appropriate it, and now at last they can look in and even do a few manipulations on the fetus, called "fetal surgery." The amazing thing is that many women, and even more the husbands, get all excited about seeing the baby inside and watching it move, as though feeling it move weren't enough. Last spring I met a woman in Sweden, a nurse whose husband is a physician. Fifteen years after the birth of her first two children, she became pregnant again, when the new techniques had become available. And because she was now "old" she was persuaded to have an ultrasound scan and amniocentesis. She hated the procedures and in retrospect feels that they made her husband form a connection with the fetus, quite independent of her in whose body the fetus was living. The fetus became his baby and she, its container.

Trying to bring the inside out and the outside in is having complicated effects. Women are put in an ambiguous position that they have trouble sorting out. When a baby has a sex and usually a name months before it is born, what does that do to the way pregnant women look upon themselves and their babies? It anticipates the process of separation that used to happen at birth and turns the fetus who until lately was unequivocally inside us and part of us into a separate person and a patient in his or her own right. This lends itself to looking on women and fetuses as disconnected, as we see in so-called surrogate motherhood, where a woman is said to carry some other people's child in her own body. (Margaret Atwood paints a horrifying picture of what that feels like in *The Handmaid's Tale.**)

I don't believe that every woman does, or needs to, feel that she is destined to be a mother. Pregnancy, birth, and motherhood are experiences that are embedded in society and history, not in nature. But one doesn't have to resort to naturalistic explanations to argue that a woman who is carrying a fetus, or a woman who has carried one for nine months and just given birth, has a different relationship to it than anyone else has. After birth, with time, her connection may weaken or even disappear, if others share in the baby's care or take it over. But initially, surely, she is in a different position from the man who has provided the sperm or the woman who has provided the egg, when the egg isn't the gestating woman's, no matter what their plans are for their future relationship to that child.

And yet, I don't want laws passed that forbid women to arrange to have babies with whomever they choose to have them. I don't think they should get paid more than their expenses and I certainly would outlaw the brokers who arrange these transactions (and are paid lots of money for their services). But much as I hate to see all these medical and social interventions in women's child-bearing, once they exist, women, and not lawyers or judges or physicians, must have the right to say yes or no.

It's late and I am tired. But I think these are really important subjects for us to be thinking about.

Much love,

Ruth

* *The Handmaid's Tale* by Margaret Atwood. Boston: Houghton Mifflin, 1986.

Letter Eight

Albuquerque, New Mexico
August 15th, 1987

Dearest Ruth:

One more letter, before heading east! That's what I always say: just one more. Your last couple of letters have given me so much to which I want to respond. First, what you say about doing what you have to do in order to be able to feel insider to yourself, inside in your own aging woman's body. That's so important, really central, and I daily feel some degree of anger at the constant struggle most of us have to wage simply in order to feel insider in ourselves!

When you look at it, it would almost seem that we are all born disabled, or inadequate to the task. And of course we're not, but from the moment of our birth (perhaps before it) we must struggle uphill as it were: against the barrage of forces lined up against us.

You make such an important point when you speak of the need to learn to listen to our bodies, and society's constant war against our being able to do that. Beginning with our parents, family doctors, and others in earliest childhood who "know what's best for baby" and begin to teach us: "Open your mouth! That's it! Eat! . . . Finish your meal! . . . Do it for mommy! (or daddy, or granma, or whomever) . . . This won't hurt (or 'it will only hurt a little')

. . . You're cold; put your sweater on! . . . You're hot; take it off! . . . Come now, you don't want to look like that! . . . Too fat . . . Too thin . . . " and all the rest.

The owners of these voices have "only our best interests" at heart (and, indeed, most of them really do, which is the saddest and most frightening part!). As we grow the voices multiply, and the chorus becomes more discordant. Teachers' expectations are added to parents'. We begin to need the acceptance of a peer group, and so whatever appearance and habits are possessed by the most popular among us become another layer of acquired needs, pulling our confusion in yet another direction. Radio and television commercials and magazine ads soon join the invading army. Many if not most of these voices become internalized as if they were our own, as if they represented what *we* need, who *we* are; and so we may be forty or fifty before we finally begin to try to sort it out, take stock of what needs to be unlearned, attempt to go back to square one. (Or we may never sort it all out.) I think it's shameful, humiliating, and enraging that in our "advanced" society most of us, as women, must literally fight for our lives to be able to *hear* our own body's voice!

I am almost fifty-one. I weigh at least forty pounds more than I should and my body feels this, knows it without doubt. In your August 7th letter you talk about addictions and your feeling that the answer is, first of all, to become an insider in your body. I couldn't agree more. The struggle seems to be one of wading through years, layers, of misdirected signals (and the deep emotional and physical scars they've left upon us) in order to return to a place where each of us can reclaim that insider space.

I'm working on it. But it's such an uphill struggle. The other day I was talking to my mother and the subject of my losing weight came up. "Don't give us anything else for Christmas," my mother said. "The best present you could give us would be if you could really lose weight!" It was meant as encouragement. And I'm aware, of course, that my mother too has been victimized by society's mixed messages around all this. (One of my daughters has problems with eating and her self-image, and every time I see her struggling with that I remember a scene I would rather forget in which her father and I fought in her four-year-old presence and she watched us, anguished, spitting up the yogurt she was trying to finish before

107

going off to nursery school. It's all too easy to make the connections.) I know full well that until we can really stop trying to look a certain way to please a social distortion, a media image, our lovers or our mothers—rather than because our bodies tell us that's what's right for us—we will continue to be outsiders to our physical selves.

Not only do I resent the uphill nature of these struggles, but the time they use and the anguish they produce. The facility with which I can analyze a television spot—and my subsequent trip to the corner to buy the advertised vitamin or skin cream. I have not used make-up for years, I dress in line with my own comfort and my love of indigenous art, and recently I've even managed to nurture (rather than remove) a garden of hair on my chin (otherwise known as a beard). But these small breakthroughs only point up the need for a really integrated coming together of the informed rebel and the woman at home in her internal space. I find I'm still working too hard on that.

I don't know if this is true for you, but when I see my children—especially my daughters—struggle endlessly around these same issues, and feel disempowered to help them in any meaningful way (knowing they've got to fight their battles as I do mine), it makes me even angrier. I began this letter wanting to write more about my children, and my insider/outsider relation to them, but got off on the above because I wanted to respond to some of the things you said.

Insider/outsider issues come up not only in the context of our own mothering, but in the context of our children's perceptions as well—how inside or out we felt or feel, vis-à-vis our offspring; how they may feel on the receiving end of our assumptions and conduct.

In your August 10th letter you talk about being in West Africa and being asked by virtually everyone, "How many children do you have?" It reminded me of my trip to Vietnam in 1974. There the usual and expected questions greeting women were, "How old are you? How many children do you have?" In that order. The question about age indicated respect. The older you were the more inside, veneration being reserved for the really ancient. Immediately after that it was: how many children do you have, assuming—as you remarked in the context of West Africa—that if you were a woman you were naturally a mother.

I was traveling with another North American woman. At that time she didn't have children; I had four. Faced with that greeting, I always felt inside because I could smile and say four. My travel companion resented the fact that she was somehow outside because she had none. Woman's identity included being a mother, although needless to say there are women in Vietnam, as there are everywhere, who are not. During that country's generations of war, one sensed that this mothering included all Vietnamese children—the children in a bombed village, the orphans, the homeless, the maimed. As with growing old, bearing children and loving children were expected conditions—and venerable ones— for women.

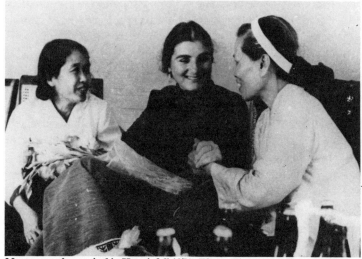

Margaret on her arrival in Hanoi, fall 1974. (Photo: Vietnamese News Agency)

An aside: in Southeast Asia I also noticed that being left-handed was seen as unusual, outside. The woman with whom I was traveling had that "stigma" as well. When she stopped in the street to take notes, crowds of kids would run up and stare at this hugely outsized female foreigner writing with the "wrong" hand! There are societies, of course, in which tradition of one kind or another is so strong that simply being like others is an insider condition; not being like others places you outside.

Your description of the insider/outsider aspects of having your children vis-à-vis just being yourself, in other words being a mother and/or being the woman (person) you are, taps into things I think about a great deal. I touched on it in my last letter, but there's always more. You did it twice, with two different experiences. I did it four times, with that many different experiences—and, perhaps not altogether strangely, I think the time I felt most myself, most insider to my own identity, was when I did it in what was supposedly the most outside way—alone; when I had Gregory.

In 1960 it was not usual for someone of my class and culture to have a child on her own, especially if she insisted, as I did, that it was not an accident. I was indeed an outsider to most of my society. But, as I say, I never felt more inside to myself. Doing it on my own meant I didn't have to deal with anyone else's ideas about children, not even a partner's, not even if the partner was also the child's father. With subsequent children I always had some sort of conflict in that area—sometimes large, sometimes small. There were differences about how children should be treated, raised, what place they should occupy in family life.

Most of this had to do with my ideas about myself, as a woman, as a person. And with the fact that it simply never occurred to me that my personhood (which most of all meant my creative self) should or could be placed second to mothering. I couldn't conceive of it seconding anything. And, although I belong to the same middle class you do, from your description of your early mothering it seems to me that I had to overcome much greater hurdles, battle my way through heavier obstacles, to be able to continue to work and create and be a mother. I didn't yet have a profession, and didn't have a daily helper until my second child was born in Mexico, and then only briefly.

The two fathers with whom I lived during and after our children were born to varying degrees expected me to be The Mother. They might help. They might or might not believe themselves extraordinary in doing so. But I never thought they should even think of themselves as "helping." For me, it was always clear that if two people take on the responsibility of having a child, they share that responsibility, equally.

Of course I'm making this seem much simpler than it was. I

neither understood this all at once, nor was I able to express it without my quota of socially-conditioned guilt. Struggles in these areas followed the general progression of my own growth into someone who knows what I need and will not make concessions around issues of principle.

Ruth, you've asked about my having Gregory without anaes-thesia, at a time when that wasn't all that common. What it was that prompted both you and me, in the late fifties and early sixties, when it wasn't yet "in," to insist on a more natural way of delivering. In New York, natural childbirth and rooming-in (the extra you had with your births) were just beginning to be talked about; I remember they were being practiced at a hospital uptown, but it was expensive, something for the elite.

I had strong feelings about what I wanted, and insisted on getting it—and I don't even know who my models were. I do remember that my obstetrician was an elderly male general practitioner; he thought I was crazy to ask about things like being conscious at my baby's delivery, breast-feeding, and other such "nonsense" (as he called it). It never occurred to me to seek another doctor. I had very little money and in any case probably would have had a hard time finding someone with my ideas. I figured out that if I refused to sign the release allowing them to anaesthetize me, I wouldn't be any worse off than centuries of women who had their kids in fields, and I'd be able to fully experience this important time. It took courage (and stamina) during twenty-five hours of labor, but that's what I ended up doing.

It was also tremendously important to me to be able to nurse my child. In the factory-like hospital in which Gregory was born, they simply fed the kids in the nursery to make things easier on the staff. By the time they brought your baby to you, he or she was fast asleep. No urge to suckle at all. My breasts became impacted and the nipples inverted from ignorance and lack of preparation and I wasn't able to nurse Gregory. I harbored an anger and resentment about that for years—until I finally understood that you could drive yourself as crazy with "what might have been and wasn't" as you could with "what could be but won't."

All I know, in retrospect, is that being awake for my first child's birth didn't end up being the heaviest insider/outsider issue. In fact, it was fairly easy to resolve. What was harder was the fact that I was unmarried, and how I was (mis)treated in that hospital because of that. For example, had I possessed a husband, he would have been allowed in my labor room. Good friends, who brought me to the hospital—and waited hours in the hall while I struggled through a difficult labor alone—were not.

I also remember indignities around race, although they didn't directly involve me. A Black woman's baby was held up by the floor nurse for everyone on the ward to see, as she laid on us all a jumbled and racist lecture on pigmentation. A Chinese woman, obviously new in this country, was loudly berated because her customs somehow conflicted with absurd hospital rules. Unwed, Black, Chinese: we were together and very outside.

Your mention of public and private schooling for your kids also rings some interesting bells. In Mexico, where three of my children began their schooling, the inside thing in our milieu was to send your kids to an active (alternative) school: Frenet, Summerhill, Montessori. We thought Mexican public schools were terrible, often the teachers—who had to work more than one job just to stay alive—didn't even show up, and of course we wanted something better for our children. I remember sending Gregory, then Sarah, and finally Ximena to a Frenet school called Manuel Bartolomé Cosío. It cost twelve dollars a month for each of them, and my parents helped pay for that.

Of course this made for political contradictions (as did having a maid and other aspects of life in Mexico). When we moved to Cuba that was the end of private schools; the entire educational system was of a socialist piece, and we chose to send the older three to *becas* (schools where the kids lived, studied, and worked during the week, coming home only on weekends). Undoubtedly, this made it much easier for me to be myself, that is to explore my creativity, write, do political work, earn a living. I also thought, at the time, that it was important for the kids: a way for them to reap the fullest benefits of a socialist education, in a totally collective environment. I believed that it had been a mistake allowing my children to attend a special school in Mexico, a schooling the vast majority of that nation's young people could not have. The move to Cuba, I thought, obliged us to correct that mistake.

My children and I have often spoken of the benefits and disadvantages in all this. When we went to Cuba the revolution was only ten years old, much was still experimental or in transition. What looked great on paper, when translated into the real-life context of, say, a fourteen-year-old teacher coping with thirty kids just five or six years his or her junior, wasn't always satisfying. In many areas the ideas were on target but their implementation left a great deal to be desired. Today residential schooling in Cuba only exists from junior high up, except in very particular circumstances.

Gregory suffered with some aspects of life in the *beca* but today generally feels it was a productive experience. Nonetheless, he chose to stay there only until his junior year of high school, when he quit the most prestigious boarding school in the country, switched to an ordinary high school, and then went on to get his college degree without the change having affected him in any but the most liberating ways.

Sarah hated boarding school all the way through, but reproached her brother for quitting; she stuck it out to the end. She now feels it did *not* benefit her. Ximena decided early on that she didn't want to continue on a boarding basis; she was a day pupil throughout junior high and high school. And Ana never went to boarding school at all; by the time it was her turn, we saw that experience as more negative than positive.

Interestingly, Sarah—the only one of my kids who remained in boarding school—is the one who has the most solidly-defined sense of self, of purpose, and of belonging to a particular place: Cuba. Gregory seems to be a case apart, as he has always had the capacity to understand his needs and potential in a particularly multifaceted way. Ximena and Ana, the two who spent more time at home, more time in the family (with that possibility for insiderness the older kids missed by being away at school) are today the two who seem to have the deepest problems in terms of finding their own insiderness.

You say that "my comfort in my own outsiderness in its different dimensions made it quite unproblematic for me to let my children . . . construct their own outsider realms . . . " I feel very close to that. It's been true for me, as well. I notice my parents, my

113

sister, and others showing concern at times for young people (especially their own children or grandchildren) when they do not follow society's prescribed norms for growing and developing. "Turning out right" is very important, and the idea of what constitutes right doesn't seem to change, essentially, over the years. If you're a boy it's important to finish school, get a good job, marry someone nice, have a family. If you're a girl the first two are important though not as important; the second two are even more so.

It's fundamental to me that my children learn to take care of

Margaret (pregnant with Sarah) and Gregory, Jalapa, Veracruz, Mexico, 1963.

themselves in this world, do it at something that gives them pleasure, and be principled in what they do. Insofar as an education helps with the first two possibilities, I want them to study. But as far as I'm concerned a craft and a profession carry the same weight.

I'm not concerned if one of my kids needs to do things in another order, or even in another way altogether; take a year or more than a year, retrace, regroup, change his/her mind. But I want them to be able to make their way, without an overdependence on others. And I see my daughters as I see my son in this respect. In fact I've always thought it more important for a woman to be able to make her own way, since middle-class society creates so many places where women can (presumably) hide and be "cared for," to our distinct disadvantage.

I, like you, am concerned when I see my kids conforming to things to which I feel no one should conform. And I'm concerned when I see them caught up in one way or another with the consumerism and other aspects of a commodity-oriented society. When they let things rule them, or—worse—see themselves as things. I don't want to see them objectified, or objectifying themselves. I would hate it if they used heavy drugs, involved themselves with shallow people, or became politically reactionary. Yet I respect them as individuals and know any one of them could conceivably become involved in something very distant from my values.

As a teenager I went through a period very alien to my parents' values and tastes when I became an Episcopalian, then a Job's Daughter, wanted to be cheerleader or Homecoming Queen. Wanted to belong. The insider thing, again, and based not on a sense of one's true inside, but upon the false and coercive models society imposes. I found my own way through that and out to the other side. Finding a way to be insider to yourself involves, I believe, a certain amount of experimentation.

At the end of your last letter, when you begin talking about insider/outsider issues in terms of pregnancy, the fetus, the woman's womb, the medical profession's sinister "advances," you're addressing problems about which we've only begun to think. In fact, most people don't think about them at all. How can we force these points of view (every pun intended!) on the policy-makers? The same story repeats itself: we get a Three-Mile Island and then a Bhopal, and still there is more protection for industrial profit than for human life. We get an epidemic like AIDS, and many are still more interested in using it to stir anti-gay fires than to fund education or medical research and support systems. Like you, I do not want to see us put more power in the hands of our governing officials; they have shown us again and again for and against whom they will use that power. Women like McKinnon and Dworkin are properly outraged at state-nurtured misogyny, but they don't seem to understand the nature of the system that rules us.

Like you, Ruth, the splits in our movement sadden (and frighten) me. We all know they benefit no one more than they do the forces that would place us, once and for all, totally outside: dead. I'll leave for another letter any ideas I might have about how to work on healing those splits. I'm written out for today.

So much love,

Margaret

Letter Nine

Woods Hole, Massachusetts
August 18th, 1987

Dearest Margaret:

I loved your last letter and want to start by responding to some of the things you said near the beginning, where you write that you "weigh at least forty pounds more than [you] should . . . " You say that your body tells you this, but you also talk about the societal messages, your mother's Christmas wish that you lose weight. So, as with my other friends who talk about being "overweight" I cannot help but wonder how much the message is in fact coming from inside your body and how much it is imposed from outside. I know it's impossible to tell. Also it is easy for me to say that, since my body happens to send me very strong signals that make it easy for me to conform to this society's fetish of slimness. And I know that it doesn't feel good to weigh too much, but what is "too much" and how can you tell? So, I continue to wonder whether it's the weight that doesn't feel good or the messages you inevitably get about it and that you choose to agree with. I guess what I am asking is this: What would happen if you said to yourself, "I don't care one bit about my weight; all I want is for my body to feel good," and then did whatever made you feel good? Would you gain weight or lose it? Obviously, "weight" is not a signal from inside; it's just a number on a scale. What are the inside signals to which you need to listen in order to feel good? It seems to me that those are what each of us needs to locate and then let the weight fall where it may (pun intended).

And now I'll be slightly less personal and talk about what it has meant to be a scientist and a professor at Harvard. But since I am talking about how I came to science and Harvard and the dynamic between my insider and outsider relationships to them, that too will end up being personal. So, as usual I'll start at the beginning, meaning in Vienna.

In high school (Gymnasium) we had chemistry and physics but no biology by the time I left. Since it was a girls' school and all the teachers were women, science was as much a girl's subject as any other. My father had loved physics in school and tried to communicate that love to me. I was not particularly excited by my science courses, but followed his lead to the extent that later, when I was offered the choice of studying chemistry or physics at Brookline High, I opted for physics. Another reason I did it was that most of my classmates took chemistry and I liked to be different. Here again, my outsiderness to the total scene made me unaware that girls were not supposed to like science and especially not physics. The course was pretty boring, but it got me to borrow books about physics from the local library. That year I read all the books for the general public that people like Einstein, Planck, Eddington, Whitehead, and Russell wrote, with the result that I entered college thinking I might major in philosophy and physics. But since I intended to go to medical school and didn't much like my first physics course in college, I chose the most popular premed major, biochemistry. Although my interest in science was mainly goal-oriented (medical school) and didn't have much to do with my love of nature, love of nature and wanting to feel part of it also influenced my decision.

Science was taught very badly at Radcliffe. The college never had a faculty of its own, but contracted for Harvard's professors (all men, of course) to teach us. In the introductory science courses,

Harvard kept the best instructors for its own (male) students and sent us newly-hired faculty who felt they were doing us a favor by coming to the boondocks. I will never forget my instructor in freshman chemistry, a young man just out of Dartmouth, who always wore his green blazer and oozed disdain. I enjoyed my science courses less than any others and didn't do as well in them. The only reason I stayed in science was that I planned to go to medical school. Finally, my last year at Radcliffe, I took a research course and began to work in George's lab and that's how I met him. He set me to work with a woman graduate student doing fairly boring things, but I loved the life of the lab, the wide-ranging discussions, the easy socializing and good times we had together. When George asked whether I'd stay on after I graduated and work on a war project with him and a younger male Ph.D., I jumped at the chance. And that's what started my life in science.

By the end of the war, when I entered graduate school, I was sure I wanted to be a scientist and not a physician, and a biologist at that. Graduate school was a very good experience and a very insider one. There were quite a few women graduate students in biology and gender was not much of an issue (at least not as far as my low level of sensibility let me notice). I frankly did not think about the fact that all the faculty was male and that I therefore had no job prospects at Harvard. All of us graduate students taught in lab courses and I didn't look beyond that. It was the same story when I worked in labs in London and Copenhagen. Women and men worked side by side, and I did not have the political acumen to notice that the positions of power and decision-making always were occupied by men. We did our work, socialized, and the atmosphere was open and friendly. I felt welcome and liked being there.

As the years passed, my work became very important to me and I derived a large part of my identity from it. There was a nice balance between working alone and collaborating with others, much discussion and debate, and much informal socializing. I liked the mix of intellectual work and getting my hands dirty. Getting a Ph.D. was a milestone I passed easily and I had no trouble getting post-doctoral fellowships. My work was enjoyable and highly regarded. I went to meetings, gave talks, wrote papers, exchanged ideas with colleagues and friends far and wide. But I was never offered a position in a university. What's more, I did not notice it. Or rather, when it was called to my attention, as colleagues sometimes did, I acted as though I had acquired my ambiguous status (insider in science, outsider in the university) by choice.

I remember saying to a man at a party, sometime around 1955, that I considered it "my prerogative as a woman" not to need to have a faculty position in order to continue working as a scientist. If I ask myself what I could possibly have meant, I think it had to do with the fact that I didn't particularly like what I saw the (male) professors doing and how they behaved with each other. I did not know any women professors, and trusted fate that I'd find a suitable niche somewhere—hopefully as a scientist though not as a professor—when I had to move on. I certainly had no picture of what it would be, what my "woman's prerogative" would lead me to *do*, rather than *not* do. I did not mean that I would marry and stop being a scientist. I was dreaming.

I continued that way until the late 1960s, when I suddenly realized that without noticing, I had slipped into a situation where my opportunity to work as a scientist had become dependent on George's being a professor; that if he left Harvard, my own position at Harvard would disappear. That had been true for a number of years, so I could have noticed it before, but until my feminist consciousness rose, I didn't face up to it. The fact of being an insider in science had been enough; I didn't notice how outside the accepted professional ladder I was. And when I did notice, my first thought was, "If I don't work in George's lab, in whose lab should I work?" (And by "lab" I didn't mean a place, but a social and economic unit, "Professor X's laboratory.") So blinded was I, such an outsider, that it took a while before I woke up to the fact that as a competent scientist and adult, I could build my own lab and did not need to find a place in someone else's. And I think that had to do with my drawing a certain comfort and security from being outside the structure; it is what I may have meant by "my prerogative as a woman"—to be outside and yet inside. Of course, I didn't have that prerogative, but it took a change in political sophistication for me to see that.

In the late 1960s, women who worked in various departments at Harvard began to meet to talk about our ambiguous positions as insiders in our fields and our work, and outsiders in the university—research fellows, research associates, instructors, lecturers. I also began to meet with a group of women professionals in the Boston area. And once we started talking, we realized that we had worked as hard and long as our male counterparts and were as good and productive in our professions, but they had real jobs and were professors, while we had quasi-positions and were outsiders who could be dropped at the flick of a pen. So, while we were insiders within our subject matter, day-to-day work, and even our professional associations, narrowly defined, we were outsiders to the organizations where we worked and where the decisions that affected our professional lives were being made.

I was lucky, because about the time I began to notice, so did some of my (of course male) colleagues in the biology department and we decided that it was past time for me to try to get recognition, meaning tenure, for the work I had been doing at Harvard. And since there was political pressure on the university to begin to hire women faculty, the university acknowledged that some of us women who had been working in various off-ladder positions should get tenure. So a few of us got professorships. The dean of the faculty and the president shook my hand. Overnight I was a member, a bona fide insider.

When my appointment was announced, an astute acquaintance wrote in her note of congratulation: "Isn't it a pity that you couldn't have got it earlier, when it would have meant so much to you." She was right because by the time I got the job, I had moved too far outside for it to matter to me in any but the practical ways—higher status, increased and secure income, better and more extensive fringe benefits. Because during the years that my appointment was winding its way through the prescribed channels, my interest in science and my appraisal of it and the university had begun to change.

Once I had acknowledged to myself that not only I, but

women as a group, had been outsiders to the relationship with nature that we call science, it became obvious to ask how our exclusion had shaped science, meaning the ways scientists conceptualize nature and the ways they describe it and use it. And once I allowed myself to ask that question, the gendered nature of science stared me in the face.

I began to see that science and technology are disciplines invented by men to dominate nature, defined as female. I also began to notice the male-biased ways scientists describe female animals and women. What is more, the image of science as austere and demanding complete devotion and around-the-clock attention from those who would practice it, clearly was built around the biographies of men, who could afford to devote all their time to the study of nature because women (their mothers, sisters, wives, daughters and servants) were taking care of their daily (and nightly) needs. The structure of the profession and its intellectual content do not reflect necessities imposed by nature, but the historical fact that scientists have been men, and economically and socially privileged men at that.

This seems obvious now, but to the true believer I was around 1970, it was shocking and revolutionary. A number of other feminists with scientific training were coming to these conclusions about the same time, but we didn't yet know each other. So, while these ideas were exciting, like any dramatically different way to see what has seemed well understood, they were also scary. There was no one to talk with about them, lots of people thought they were crazy, and they threatened my identity as a scientist. I remember waking up in a sweat in the middle of the night thinking, if I'm not a scientist, who am I?

Now we have a flourishing field of feminist science criticism, with exciting books, meetings, and conferences. We have generated a new inside, but most scientists look on us as outsiders. Many of us, ourselves, do not. I still think of myself as a scientist because I am as interested as ever in getting to understand nature. But I have come to feel that the science that is being practiced is on the wrong track and is leading us away from that understanding rather than toward it. An outsider vision, no?

To what extent am I choosing to be an outsider? To what extent do I gain strength from that in science and the university? Implicit in that question is the assumption that I could be an insider if I were willing to make the necessary compromises to fit "their" image of what being a scientist and Harvard professor means. Certainly it hasn't always been true, but I believe that since I have had tenure my colleagues would happily treat me as an insider if I played by their rules—did their kind of science, taught their kinds of courses and did it in their way (lecturing, testing, grading, encouraging competition, and so on).

Ruth lecturing in Switzerland, 1975.

There is no question that I get a sense of empowerment from having worked my way inside and then decided that it's not where I want to be. It's quite different from not having that choice. But why not get out? Why be a quasi-inside outsider? That has to do with the practical advantages and falls in the category of manipulating the system. It is not heroic, but enables me to be more effective with my students and some of my colleagues, and politically outside the university.

In a recent conversation you suggested that if I stay, it means that it's where I want to be. I don't think that's true. I don't want to be a Harvard professor in the same sense in which I don't want to be in Reagan's America. In both cases, I stay because I recognize that I need to make certain compromises because of the other things I want to do.

At the time I decided to try to get tenure, and to stay if I got it, the alternative was to leave and begin from scratch in some other setting. That would have required its own compromises and would not have let me get as far as quickly or given me as much freedom of movement as quickly. So, realizing that, I wanted to stay. But there are many counter-arguments. One, of course, is that I don't enjoy working at Harvard and sometimes hate it, and that is a drain/strain. (One of my Marxist friends—a white, male Harvard professor—argues that, after all, most people don't enjoy where they work and that's a perfectly reasonable compromise to make. I'm not sure.) The other, more serious point, as far as the things I believe in and work for is concerned, is that my being a Harvard professor, and doing and saying the things I do, strengthens the official image of Harvard as a liberal institution that makes a place for all kinds of people and beliefs. It does nothing of the sort! A few of us manage to sneak in. If they could get rid of us without marring their image as a liberal institution, they gladly would, but they are powerful enough to be able to afford a few of us.

There's a further problem. I firmly believe that educational institutions like Harvard exist to train people for service to the corporate state. So, teaching in any of them requires that we get sufficient power to be able to subvert the intent of the exercise for ends of liberation, real analysis and understanding, positive action, etc. I can use my position at Harvard for ends that I believe in and to help people whom I want to help, but I can imagine a life that I'd feel more in tune with on many levels. In fact, I've often thought of going to work for an organization like the American Friends Service Committee after I retire, so that I can have the experience of being genuinely invested in what I do.

In a way, you can make a similar argument. If you win your INS case, it will be used by some as proof that "the system works," "the courts work," "justice prevails." Whereas you shouldn't have to be going through what you are going through if the system really worked.

One of the bad things about feeling as alienated and outside as I do at Harvard is that my relations with students have deteriorated. I no longer make the effort to get through to those whom I classify (no doubt sometimes unjustly) as fitting comfortably into the official structure and its make-believe. I reach out only to students who I sense are uncomfortable. Yet, when people ask what I do, I say I am a teacher. In part, that's because it's a quick and easy answer. A couple of years ago I heard a man referred to as a social critic, and decided that would be a good thing to call myself. But even without that, I get into enough trouble if people then ask, "What do you teach?" I usually say "biology," because that's easy. Then because I can't bring myself to leave it at that, I add "and women's studies," and then comes "what's that?"

So I'm a teacher; but I wouldn't say that I love to teach and I've never understood why not. The fact is I find teaching stressful, having to perform, be the focus of attention. It's a demand to which I don't respond easily. I am much more comfortable in one-on-one situations. When I do have to face a crowd, I find a one-shot deal—arrive, lecture, leave—much easier than teaching with its need to prepare a syllabus, reading lists, the weekly exigencies. For years, and much to my students' exasperation, I have met my class once a week for two and a half hours rather than the more conventional one and a half hours twice a week, because I can't face having to meet them twice a week. What's that about? I am a teacher. I quite enjoy it. Call myself that. But I feel sort of outside even there and can't do it in the standard format. Not to speak of doing it like a Harvard professor, which I can't do because I want not only to share power but to use my teaching to *empower* students and get them to comprehend the cultural and personal sources of their disempowerment and overcome them.

Maybe it would be easier to teach a less privileged group of students. (It'll be interesting to see how you feel about Trinity vs. the University of New Mexico). But of course in the United States even privileged kids feel disempowered. (One year I had the daughter of an important official in the administration in Washington—she said to me, "He has so much power and he is so terrible!" She nearly died of anorexia in her teens and now, in her

125

twenties, is constantly on the edge of breaking bones from osteoporosis. This is one kind of privilege I see.) They, too, need to sort out who they want to be and can be (*they* have choices) and how they want to live their lives in a morally and politically responsible way. So to be the kind of teacher I want to be I have to be an outsider in my institution where each year a special office mails out statistics to tell us how our course compares to others in terms of grade distribution (the aim being not to give too many high grades) and whether the students rate it as competitive (they of course should feel great pressure to compete), and similar junk. I throw that mailing away along with most mailings I get from the administration and from my department. But again that means I'm an outsider.

Another issue comes up here in Woods Hole. When I started coming here it was to work at the Marine Biological Laboratory (M.B.L.). It is a private corporation, owned by scientists and run by an administration that has become bureaucratic and overgrown like most administrations. I am a member of the corporation and used to go to the annual meeting. During the 1970s, for five years, I was even a trustee and went to biannual trustees' meetings, served on committees, and helped run the place. To all that, I now feel a complete outsider, partly because I am no longer interested in the science these people do and partly because I have very little else in common with them and don't even like most of them. Most of them are men and don't think or talk about much other than their work. There are a few women scientists I like and talk with. But I am an outsider to the scientific Woods Hole I first came to.

There's something else to say here. I don't regret this distancing of myself and don't feel bad about it. I don't feel excluded. In fact, I have the illusion that if I got interested in again doing their kind of science, my colleagues in the department and in Woods Hole would welcome me back. I rather think it makes them uncomfortable to see someone lose interest the way I have done. Most academics are insecure people who flee into the universities because they aren't sure they can survive in the "real world." When someone opts out, it raises worrisome questions for them. So I think they'd be glad if I came back in.

126

I guess what I am saying is that in the university and in science the boundary between insider and outsider for me is permeable. In most respects, I am not one or the other. Almost always I am both and can use both to develop material, intellectual, and political resources and construct insider enclaves in which I can live, love, work, and be as responsible as I know how to be. So, once more I am back to the dynamic between insider and outsider and the strengths that we can gain from their simultaneous coexistence and that surprises and interests me a lot.

Much love,

Ruth

Letter Ten

Woods Hole, Massachusetts
August 20th, 1987

Dear Margaret:

There is something I want to add to the letter I wrote you the other day about feeling that I am an outsider among my colleagues in science and especially my immediate colleagues in the Harvard biology department. It has to do with the way scientific work is structured and with the content of my discipline.

As I wrote you, one of the things that attracted me to scientific work was its collective nature and the social life of the laboratory. But given the realities of academic life, the need to publish, and the competition for promotion, credit for what goes on in the laboratory tends to go to the chief, the professor, who is usually a man. Even when publications list the names of everyone who has participated in the work, the person with the well-known name gets credited by his (or her) colleagues and the others tend to be erased. Individuals cannot really correct this by being fair within their private enclaves. The hierarchical structure of the university is at fault.

During the late 1960s and early 1970s, when progressive and activist scientists were debating these issues, some tried to form laboratory collectives. But just about all of them broke down because where they had to interface with university administrations and funding agencies, these insisted that there be a "head" or "director," someone responsible for running the laboratory and administering its funds. This meant that person—usually the professor—had to assume greater responsibilities than anyone else for the direction of the work, for its results, and for generating the funds so it could continue. With that, the worm was in the apple. Genuine equality in the division of manual and mental work and in distributing the various responsibilities for carrying it out became impossible. Squabbles developed, factions appeared, and the more egalitarian structures broke down.

This is why most of us feminist scholars and science critics maintain that we cannot begin to think realistically about what an egalitarian, or feminist, science would be like as long as science is done in a hierarchical and male-dominated society. We can analyze the effects the present inequalities have and describe the gendered science that results, and we can try to mitigate such effects. But we have trouble even envisioning the radical transformations that could happen in a more egalitarian and feminist society, not to speak of bringing them about.

As to the present content of my discipline, I am an outsider to it because much of science, and especially biology, is what we call reductionist. What that means is that most biologists nowadays believe that we cannot come to understand living organisms without taking them apart. The metaphor of the organism as a machine dominates our science. The idea is that our understanding of nature, and of organisms as part of it, depends on learning everything we can about the tiniest particles in the universe. (Notice that they are called "fundamental" particles and that physics, the branch of science that studies them, is considered the most "fundamental" and prestigious branch of science.) One way to describe reductionism, as it is practiced, is to say that to understand atoms we must understand the ultimate particles within them; to understand molecules, the atoms of which they are composed; to understand organisms, we must learn about the organs and molecules within them; to understand societies, we must learn about the biology of the people who live in them. It is a bottom-up, hierarchical theory.

You learn about each successive level by gaining a better under-standing of the one below it. This is the reigning, insider paradigm in modern biology and it is the reason why genetics and genes get so much play. The idea is that to know about people you have to know all you can about our genes.

I and a number of other biologists think that this is all wrong. We hold to a more dialectical view and believe that what happens at each level—if we are to talk about a hierarchy of levels at all—must be studied at that level. Physicists and chemists cannot predict the properties of water from knowing the atomic properties of hydro-gen and oxygen. Similarly, we cannot predict what properties molecules or organs will exhibit when they interact in an integrated way inside the organism. And of course you realize that we cannot predict how a society will behave from studying the psychology or biology of the people who live in it. To coin a phrase: "The whole is greater than the sum of its parts." Genes may contribute to who we are and how we behave, as do a lot of other chemical, as well as physiological and social structures and events. But none of them "determines" us. And if we want to improve people's health and our lives, there are lots more important things to do than to identify and analyze all our genes. However, the present chairman of my depart-ment has staked his reputation and financial success on doing just that.

So, since most of my immediate colleagues are at the very heart of contemporary genetic reductionism and have not only profes-sional, but also economic investments in it, since just about all of them are principals or consultants of biotechnology companies, I am an outsider in my department. This does not mean that I am alone in my scientific and political opposition to this kind of work. I have scientific colleagues and political allies. We have formed organizations such as the Committee for Responsible Genetics and a number of feminist groups that deal with the impact of this line of work on women in the realm of prenatal screening and what is coming to be called gene therapy. In other words, I am not isolated. We have our insider world here, too, but to be able to generate it and be effective in it, we become outsiders in our academic professions.

It took me a while, after I began to think critically about science, to realize the extent to which those in power rely upon science to justify the status quo. Science is used to validate every-thing from our understanding of the cosmos to the quality of toothpaste. Most scientists deliver the representations and analyses of nature that are prized and rewarded by the corporate centers that sustain their work (including the universities, private industry, and funding agencies). In its crudest form, this is what leads some scientists to "prove" that Blacks as a group are by nature less intelligent than whites, that women (read *white* women) are by nature weaker, or less good at analytical thinking, than men, and most recently that prostitutes (read *Black women*) are spreading AIDS among heterosexuals. Although other scientists usually argue against these "scientific truths," here as in politics, official recognition and rewards, with their attending publicity, usually go to those who affirm the rightness and justice of the established distribution of power.

And I am not only thinking of such obviously ideology-riddled examples as these. There are subtler ways in which the view that nature is nothing more than a complex arrangement of cogs and wheels lends itself to the arrogant appropriation and exploitation of the earth and its atmosphere, the moon and planets, and now "outer space." As you know, the awe I feel for nature is not based on a belief in supernatural forces. I find material reality sufficiently awe-inspiring. The point is that I am convinced that a more respectful approach, one that values the complexity and integrity of nature, will yield understanding that is less disruptive and destructive of nature than the science and technology now being practiced.

I am not trying to lead us into a lengthy discussion of science or a comparison of our philosophies of nature. But I felt that my last letter did not touch on some of the things that most alienate me from the science my colleagues practice.

Much love,

Ruth

Letter Eleven

Hartford, Connecticut
August 25th, 1987

Dearest Ruth:

Sarah brought me a letter from an old friend, a Cuban poet named Victor. His letter, for me, has brought up some heavy insider/outsider memories.

I lived in Cuba from the fall of 1969—with some extended absences for travel—until the end of 1980. I was a North American, coming from this country whose successive governments had by that time tried by every possible means to destroy the Cuban revolution. Yet I felt I was seen and treated as an individual: someone who had great respect for what the Cubans were doing, and wanted to live among them for a number of years, sharing their problems and taking part in their experimental solutions.

I know I have written in previous letters about some aspects of those years. I mentioned insisting, along with only one other family I knew at the time, on using an ordinary rather than a foreigner's ration book. I got a regular job, to which I went daily—first by bus, and when we were able to get one, in an old broken-down car. My children experienced the different types of Cuban education, ranging from early day care through college.

We shared our living quarters when it was clear that housing was the single most oppressive problem in that society. We took our health problems to an evolving medical system, in which access was free for everyone and progress happened horizontally rather than vertically. In short, I tried—as I have done everywhere—to be an insider in a situation I appreciated and supported. If I repeat some pieces of this here, it's to emphasize once more how very inside I felt.

That inside situation was not without cracks. For example, as foreigners we could travel whenever and wherever we wanted. The currency exchange situation made it very difficult, if not impossible, for most Cubans to do the same, and this caused resentment, becoming perhaps the single most important problem pushing some to emigrate.

As recent arrivals, we had been given a large apartment, in line with the size of our family (the Cuban Revolution's goal for everyone.) But thousands of families still grew as extensions to the man's or woman's family of origin; housing by the time we moved there was already a real problem.

Although none of my children ever complained that they were treated differently because they weren't Cuban, my son Gregory sometimes shared stories of the subtle differentiation he felt when for one reason or another his earned insiderness came up against a classmate's perception of his Yankee origin.

But something happened during those Cuban years, an "event" about which I've spoken and written almost not at all, which definitely heightened my outsider feelings.

Even putting the word "event" in quotes says something about the strange and difficult nature of the experience. For this was not something defined as an event might be, not something with a palpable beginning or end, in fact not something easy to disentangle or discuss. It was something it may never be entirely possible to understand. Nonetheless, in the context of our discussion I feel the need to write about it now.

In 1975, after having worked for six years in Cuba's publishing industry; after having had scores of poems, articles, essays, and translations published in Cuban journals; after having participated in a number of intellectual projects, judged literary contests, engaged in public debates, and in general been accepted into the cultural and intellectual life of the country, I suddenly lost my job.

Margaret during a break from interviewing for *Cuban Women Now*, Bayamo, Cuba, 1970. (Photo: Mayra A. Martinez)

I asked my immediate superior what was going on, but found his answers vague and unacceptable. I went to my trade union. The grievance officer was sympathetic, but nothing happened to clarify the situation. I gradually went higher and higher, attempting to discover—with increasing frustration—why I had been cut out of my workplace. No luck. Most of those to whom I went showed initial surprise, were sure there was some mistake, would get back to me right away—and then didn't. A few of these people were courageous and outspoken enough to agree that something wasn't right, but eventually they were no more help than their more cautious comrades.

As I knocked on door after door, I became more and more anguished. I felt isolated. A few "friends" stopped coming around. I couldn't get another job. In some important ways my insider situation was turning inside out.

Yet—and this was perhaps the most confusing aspect of the whole situation—I continued to draw a paycheck every month. I sent my poems and articles to magazines and papers where they continued to find a warm reception. In 1978, a book of mine long scheduled with Casa de las Americas, Cuba's most prestigious publishing house, came out in a lovely edition.

Some people suggested that I simply sit back and enjoy a situation many would find fulfilling: continuing to earn an adequate wage while having all the time I needed for my own work. But this is a problem in a socialist state; how do you define your own work? You have your personal projects, of course, but building something together involves everyone's primary and prideful labor. Although I wrote a number of books during those four or five years—as I had in the years before—the unanswered questions continued to haunt me. Why had I been laid off without an acceptable explanation? Why couldn't I get a straight answer from anyone? What had I done, or failed to do, and why couldn't someone tell me about it?

In capitalism there is a growing tabulated and untabulated unemployment rate; people need and expect to work, and welfare services for those who can't find jobs are being cut back. At the same time, many (like myself during the New York years) are delighted when we can draw unemployment insurance if it gives us time to write.

Under socialism there is little if any unemployment; the right to work is the most basic right. This is true on an individual level because it's how people fulfill their needs. It's also true in a collective sense, because people are working very tangibly together to construct the world of their choice. In a worker's society, the most painful outsider experience is that of not being permitted to work. My problem finding a job in Cuba lasted, as I say, for several years. That made it even harder.

Now I want to talk about some of the conclusions I've come to as to the possible reasons for all this.

I was a North American. In Cuba, this was always an important part of who I was. (I found your reference to the students from different countries attending separate schools on Isle of Youth an interesting one. You were right, the reason for the separate schools was precisely the respect the Cubans have for different histories and cultures, and the need people have to understand and retain them.) The more sophisticated Cubans understood the complex overlays of meaning in my condition as a North American. Some who were less sophisticated probably were only able to feel it as a thorn in their sides. Revolutions, as is true of all societies, are made up of vastly different types of people, with vastly differing capacities to deal with complex issues.

I was a feminist, increasingly a very outspoken and insistent one. My feminism, informed by my North American tradition and my Latin American experience, was often provocative, hard-hitting, demanding. Again, some understood my concerns in this regard; others I'm sure resented them.

I was a woman. I don't believe there is yet a society in which women are totally accepted as equals. Cuba has gone a long way towards making this happen, but she has a long way to go. Strong women, opinionated women, women who seem to ignore the fact that they are women (within the male definition of what the condition should be), often prove unacceptable. Perhaps, as a strong and opinionated woman I was unacceptable to some.

I was a foreigner. Xenophobia is complex. Internationalism is certainly one of the most significant and powerful of the many gifts the Cuban Revolution has given to humanity. (The Cuban concept of internationalism would be, in itself, another useful subject for insider/outsider discussion.) But again, not everyone is at the same place in their grasp of the concept; nor in their ability to put it into practice.

Nineteen-seventy-five was a year when many Cubans, sent to other parts of the world for training in a variety of fields, came home to put their newly-acquired skills to work. Perhaps, in the light of this reverse migration, my work needed to be seen as superfluous—with no one brave enough to explain to me how a general phenomenon translated into an individual life. Or perhaps a single person with sufficient authority decided I should be replaced by a Cuban, and enough among the others I went to were afraid to question that authority. This time, for me, was drawn-out and oppressive. Not knowing is in itself a powerful form of oppression.

Some suggested I leave Cuba at different points during those difficult years. I never wanted to do that until the situation was explained in some way. I kept trying to find out. People kept promising to find out for me. Nothing essentially changed. And I continued to live, and work, as fully as I could.

It's important to understand the difference between this sort of thing happening in places like Cuba and the United States. In the former you are being excluded by people like yourself, people with whom—whatever your individual differences—you are building something. You become an outsider to those with whom you identify. In the latter there is always that more traditional sense of we and they; we are the people, they are a governing structure with which we have long since lost a sense of connection. If we are jobless, we are outsiders to the system, but insiders among a growing number of people for whom the system does not work. (Witness the current homeless phenomenon, in which the system's exclusion of huge numbers of people begins to say more about the nature of that system than about the nature of those who make up the new group; and so, to a certain extent at least, the homeless themselves constitute an inside.)

When you're isolated in a place like Cuba (or from a group of friends, a social group, a political nucleus, a family of whatever kind) you feel alone and hurt, the way you describe being made to feel by some of your erstwhile sisters in the women's movement.

137

When you're isolated from officialdom in this country, you share a worthy space with other dissenters and protesters: people working for a fairer people's representation, for more meaningful concepts of freedom, for equality, against the rape of earth and air, for an end to a variety of oppressions, for peace.

There was another consideration in my waiting and wanting to struggle through this problem, another consideration in my not wanting to leave Cuba until I felt the air had cleared. Many people on the left tend to expect perfection from revolutions. They take mistakes, on whatever scale, as evidence that all is lost. It's a facile way to avoid the responsibility of support and the acknowledgment that social change is complex and difficult.

And on the right, you know how quickly the U.S. propaganda machine picks up on problems of this type and publicizes them as proof that "socialism doesn't work." Events taken out of context feed preconceived doubts and prejudices. I had always tried to create bridges of understanding between the North and the South, capitalism and socialism, open-minded people in my country of origin and the political experiments of the so-called Third World. (Or, as June Jordan so aptly calls it, the First World!)*

I tried to place things in context. I was as vehemently against Cuba's portrayal of the North American society as predominantly composed of Mafia, crooked politicians, and drug dealers as I was against the United States' attempt to portray Cuba as a totalitarian state. I was always trying to put each society in context for the other, and promote understanding of a complex richness rather than of a one-dimensional caricature. And I didn't want to become, in any way, a person to whom enemies of the revolution might point and say: "See, she went to Cuba. And look what happened!"

Eventually, I was satisfied that I would probably never have a complete or detailed explanation for what had occurred. But I was able to see that I needed to accept the fact that the puzzle did indeed have many pieces. Most of them probably had more to do with the country's general situation than with me as an individual. Some undoubtedly had to do with my particular way of being, but did not—for all of that—indicate a series of official judgments from which I, or anyone else, could not dissent.

* *On Call* by June Jordan. Boston: South End Press, 1985.

I spoke long and honestly with several Cubans. I made sure that everyone (including myself) understood that in going to Nicaragua I was not "leaving" Cuba. The unanswered questions were elucidated to the best of everyone's ability. And I moved to Managua late in 1980.

Now I want to return to Victor's letter. In it, among other things, he says: " . . . I'm not engaging in mere formality when I tell you that people here are attentive to your struggle. That open hostility once directed against you—and at us, your friends, and yes, why not say it, your students—is a thing of the past. Things have changed here beyond our wildest dreams. What a wonderful thing it would be if you were able to return and spend some new time with us . . . "

Years after the events, Victor's letter reminds me that I was not alone. A small group of young poets, writers, and others always stuck by me. As long-time friends they trusted me and knew where I was coming from. As creative intellectuals, they also knew that my ideas—threatening to some—would eventually be commonplace in a society that is never static. They, in their own ways, took the risks along with me. And they were revolutionary Cubans. They had no intention of leaving their country. Whatever the battles, they would see them through where they were.

Hettie Cohen's words—this time in reverse—reverberate once more in my ears: "You dealt with it by leaving; I dealt with it by staying."

All of this, of course, reaffirms what you say in one of your early letters, that it seems to you "every culture defines what is appropriate and necessary to be an insider." You're right. The difference here in the United States, as you say, is that things are mystified in very complex and refined ways because the mystification, in its sophistication, is often subliminal and there is that pretense of freedom of choice so essential to the "Free World" myth.

Were I to have publicized my Cuban employment problem back then, choruses here would have risen in attack, choruses well-orchestrated by the establishment and echoed as well by sectors within the left. Without any knowledge of context, my problem would have been blamed on a system.

Some of these same voices say people here who can't get work are "lazy." The individual is at fault, not the system. Freedom of choice in capitalism often means the freedom to choose hunger. Attention to the collective rather than to the individual under socialism sometimes means an individual will get caught in the cogs of the wheels of change, while the texture of life for the group slowly but surely improves.

Insider/outsider considerations that in my life have crossed boundaries of place, culture, political definition.

Much much love,

Margaret

Letter Twelve

Hartford, Connecticut
September 8th, 1987

Dearest Ruth:

I want to look at the insider/outsider issues connected with my immigration case. As good a way as any to begin might be with an incident that took place just before I left Albuquerque to come east.

My housemate Barbara, my daughter Sarah, a friend named Dorothy and I went to the movies one night. "My Life as a Dog" was the Swedish film we chose to see—mostly very poignant, interesting. We'd parked the car a few blocks from the theater—we had some pizza together first—and we were walking along the sidewalk, on Central down by the university campus, when a young man in front of a bar turned as we passed.

Since the case became public property, so to speak, this kind of person's body language never goes unnoticed. Being spit at by total strangers has become almost as much a part of my life as a stranger running up to shake hands, or even hug me, and wish me well. You learn to be ready—whatever that means!—and going to the post office or to a movie isn't the same kind of private experience it once was.

This particular guy removed a pair of dark glasses in a

pointedly grandiose gesture; I can still see the glow of the evening street lamp shining on the particular whiteness of his skin as he turned from the direction in which he had been walking and stood there, trying to stare us down. As none of us immediately acknowledged the way in which he attempted to engage us, he began to shout—at first just a few sparse phrases, almost under his breath; then, when those brought no response, his voice rose, calling out epithets at our fading backs. Of course it was about me.

The shouts became more insistent, and more vehement: "Dirty commie: get out of here, go on back to Nicaragua . . . !" and probably more, that I could neither hear nor wanted to. Half a block away Barbara turned and stared him down. He couldn't sustain her gaze. His shouts became grumblings, and he turned again as if to enter the bar. We left the street and went on into the theatre.

Most Americans, of whatever political ideology, would probably tell you they want a free country, and conservatives would at least verbally agree with liberals and progressives that freedom must include the freedom to hold dissenting ideas. In practice, many rigid conservatives have decided that inside includes only people like themselves; all others are outside and should be treated as such.

After that incident on the sidewalk, we did nothing, apparently, but buy our tickets, stop at the water fountain, find seats, settle in to see the movie. But each of us—Barbara, Sarah, Dorothy, myself—in our own way held the scene in our bodies, closed our bone and muscle around it, tried not to allow it to taunt our skin throughout the film. Later during the drive home. And hours into the night.

This kind of incident, momentary as it may be, insignificant (insofar as it usually represents the lunatic fringe of a mostly indifferent public), is a powerful and all-too-frequent reminder of my outsiderness as constructed by my having chosen to defy INS deportation, governmental animosity, vindictiveness, and harassment. My insisting that I have a right to be inside, even while refusing to go back on opinions considered outsider by some.

As I've said, there are also incidents of positive public support. Much more often than this negative display, people come up to tell me they appreciate my struggle and wish me well. Although welcome, even these friendly gestures are uncomfortable at times. They, too, make it impossible for me to walk down the street in the anonymity that is lost when you become a focus of public attention.

But, of course, it is the gesture of attack—verbal, even physical at times—that most forcefully tells me I am an outsider, forever threatened by conservative hysteria, always the possible target of some madman (or woman, yes, there are those too) who may choose to deposit his or her personal frustrations against this bull's eye offered up to a manipulated and media-oriented public opinion. (And, lunatic or not, they are always portents of real danger. You may remember the case of the entire family in Seattle murdered a few years ago by a madman who later justified his act by claiming they were "communists.")

If these incidents were limited in time and space, they would lose most of their power to harass. But their effect lingers, long after the particular scene has dissolved behind one's eyes. And their power is cumulative. Far into the night, we were still discussing what had happened, how it had made us feel, how not to allow such events to corrode our peace of mind (and body), self confidence, the ability to enjoy an evening out.

For practical purposes, we made the distinction between verbal and physical threats. We felt we should probably respond to the first by pretending to ignore it. A concrete, frontal defense seemed more appropriate in fending off the second. But even these considerations, important as they may be, are largely useless in dealing with how this kind of behavior makes you feel.

The threatening letter. The threatening phone call. The sudden hostility on the part of someone who writes a letter to the editor or calls in to a talk show. The more subtle (but perhaps even more wearing) presence—who may it be? you cannot know—in a classroom, at a lecture. Accuracy in Academia. The Young Republicans. Tradition in Action. The Ku Klux Klan. Knowing your phone is tapped. Knowing "they" are tampering with your mail. Just knowing there is a "they," that never-quite-identified presence just out of sight, out of reach, out of range. (The Center for Constitutional Rights has compiled a thirty-page list of break-ins and harassment of different types against progressive political organizations, abortion clinics, and Sanctuary churches in this country just over the past several months.)

They are constantly defining us as outside. And trying to get us to define ourselves in that way. And our most consistent act of daily resistance involves struggling against that.

For all the tradition of justice in this country, for all the very real avenues of legal struggle open to the person who has the opportunity and the means to engage in this type of battle, the psychological warfare implicit in character assassination, red-baiting, womanizing, and the free and open-ended manipulation of public opinion, all make the person identified as outsider the object of attack. The government lawyers themselves, during my 1986 deportation hearing in El Paso, led the way in these provocations and smear tactics.

To be able to keep our insiderness in this context. To be able to retain our self-image, and the knowledge that we are struggling for truth—this is a very important part of what it comes down to when you're embroiled in a case like mine.

Retaining my self-image isn't always easy. Often when the case gets particularly wearing or difficult, when the difficulties affect my family or friends, I hear myself saying, "I'm really sorry . . . " as if it were my fault. As women we learn early to blame ourselves. It takes consciousness to remember it's not *my* fault but the fault of those trying to deport me.

In my last letter I explored the insider/outsider aspects of having lost my job in Cuba. It might be useful, as well, to talk about what this summer has been like, in terms of working here.

To set the scene, I should preface this by saying I am engaged in a legitimate process of appeals, currently still within the INS administrative court system. When those are exhausted, the case goes into the federal court system, with its lengthy appeals process.

I entered this country on a valid visa and have proceeded throughout in compliance with the law. Up until June of this year, immigration legislation gave me the right to work simply based on the fact that I have a number of first category relatives who are U.S. citizens. I asked for work authorization not because I had to, but as a courtesy. It was extended until just before my El Paso hearing, when on the INS director's whim it was denied, presumably so the government attorneys could bolster their weak case against me with the allegation that I was working without permission. The judge himself took note of that charge by allowing it "one scintilla of importance."

In June the immigration law changed. As part of the so-called amnesty, a band-aid attempt to deal with the problems caused by the enormous amount of immigration, Congress passed a law by which employers may now be sanctioned for hiring people who are neither citizens nor have work authorization. As a result, a number of crops have not been harvested and have rotted in the fields. Industry is losing a labor force it has exploited for years. The new law is proving to be a boomerang on a number of levels. Congress is already attempting to extend the execution date for sanctions.

But this new situation has given INS a context in which to harass me (and many others) further.*

* My immigration case proceeds along two tracks: Randall v. Meese, which challenges the INS District Director who used his discretion in denying my application for adjustment of status (I am joined in this affirmative suit by a number of well-known writers); and INS's deportation proceedings against me. The former was dismissed by District court Judge John Penn because he claimed I obtained adequate review of the denial when Immigration Judge Martin Spiegel ruled against me (not in discretion, but on the statute) in March, 1986. That decision was appealed to the U.S. Court of Appeals for the District of Columbia where oral argument was heard February 4, 1988. The deportation decision was appealed to the Board of Immigration Appeals (BIA). However, just before Christmas, 1987, Congressman Barney Frank, Senator Daniel Patrick Moynihan and others added Section 901 to State Department budgetary legislation, and it was signed into law January 1, 1988. Section 901 states that anyone who applies to enter the country during 1988 cannot be denied a visa on ideological grounds. So in early January we filed a motion with the BIA arguing that 901 applies to me, and I should therefore be granted residency. On February 4, 1988 the INS informed both the BIA and the U.S. Court of Appeals for the District of Columbia that it believes 901 applies to me. It is now up to the BIA either to grant my residency, or to remand the case to the immigration judge for him to do so. Randall v. Meese has yet to be decided. If the Court holds that jurisdiction was proper in the U.S. District Court, this, in and of itself will be a very important victory for all who seek review of a District Director's denial of adjustment of status. If the U.S. Court of Appeals further holds that the District Director's decision was unconstitutional (as we say it was), and that I should be accorded permanent resident status retroactively, that would be a great victory. As Section 901 expires at the end of 1988, it will be necessary for Congress to either extend it or make its enactment permanent. Congressman Barney Frank has legislation pending that would do away with the unconstitutional clauses of McCarran-Walter. The struggle against ideological exclusion continues until this legislation is passed. My own struggle also continues until I am granted residency. In a separate action, I am also asking that my U.S. citizenship be restored on grounds that I was not properly informed when I lost it.

I was offered a prestigious chair for the 1987-88 academic year in the English Department at Trinity College in Hartford. I began to look forward to a period of some kind of working normalcy—at least for nine months. (I had been running myself ragged teaching for little money on renewable contracts at the University of New Mexico, flying around the country to give readings and lectures, scrounging for book royalties and selling photographs, all while publicizing my case and attempting to keep up with my own ongoing work.)

But INS got wind of the offer, and its highest-ranking Albuquerque area official got on television to publicly threaten Trinity if they hired me.

The situation, which had begun with the usual interview, offer, and acceptance, became one in which no one knew what to do. New laws are never easy to interpret. The Trinity Board of Trustees hired a law firm and paid it to judge me hireable or unhireable. They in turn conferred with my lawyers, who are supported by the country's most authoritative immigration experts in their opinion that I must be considered a citizen until such time as the courts finally judge me not to be or my appeal process is exhausted.

The summer proceeded along its hot and uncertain way.

Then it was close to the end of July. I still didn't know where— or whether—I would be employed in the fall. My department chair at the University of New Mexico generously put off canceling the classes I was scheduled to teach there. Meanwhile, the people at Trinity were still waiting for word from their legal counsel.

It wasn't until the last week in July—three weeks before I needed to head east!—that this situation was brought to a more or less satisfactory conclusion: Trinity's costly legal counsel never did go out on a definitive limb, my *pro bono* law team did the actual mind and leg work, an insistent department chair at Trinity (supported by some pretty vehement positions on the part of other Trinity faculty) took a courageous stand, and the school finally agreed to extend a limited contract.

With only a few days left before school would begin, I had to finish preparing my course syllabi, get someone to stay in my Albuquerque home, leave my elderly parents, find a place to live in

Hartford, and plan for the trek across the country. The full effects of this harassment surfaced in the days immediately following the resolution. I had to deal with suppressed indignation, rage, fear, a feeling of invisibility and worthlessness.

Coming out of the Courthouse in El Paso, Texas, March 1986. Left to right: Helene Vann, Margaret, daughter Ana. (Photo: Jack Levine)

Outsider vis-à-vis any semblance of a normal life. Outsider even in the space provided by the highly advertised U.S. justice system—which surely cannot want a person to become a ward of the state while going through a legal process of appeal. But most of all, outsider to myself: forced to engage relentlessly in the struggle to trust even my capacity to work and maintain a modicum of self-worth and dignity.

Insider, of course and still, in my convictions—both as regards the defense of my freedom to dissent and my commitment to the political stand this case implies. We've spoken of the tension between insider and outsider, the ways in which this tension itself is often what moves us forward. Keeping that going in all this is a daily task for me! Their aim seems to be to use this tension against me, to wear me down and out. My task is to turn that around. It takes a great deal of energy, all the time.

Love,

Margaret

Letter Thirteen

Hartford, Connecticut
September 15th, 1987

Dearest Ruth:

Traveling, being in unfamiliar places, being mobile (or superfluous, as the case may be) has very forcefully focused my attention on the absence of that energy axis we've talked about. I often feel neither particularly insider nor outsider, belonging or alien. Not finding the axis often means not feeling that I have a choice. We have been articulating insider/outsider considerations, and I at least have tended to think of these in pretty polarized terms: either inside or out. Or inside and out at the same time. Being at loose ends in so many ways this past month or so has prodded me to reflect on the outsider quality in a variety of half-way situations: what happens when you are not completely in, or totally out.

If we know who we are, no matter what that may be, we have a sense of comfort, a certain familiarity, even a certain security. Even if we are talking about a person with AIDS, or a homeless person (two categories which have found their way into our conversation from time to time but which we have been reluctant to discuss in these letters essentially because neither you nor I are homeless, nor have AIDS), the reality no doubt is terrifying at first. Immediately you have no choice but to live with it. How inside or outside you then are, depends largely upon your ability to retain your sense of self within the given reality. That ability, in and of itself, can constitute a kind of insider state.

Barbara and I spoke about this recently in New York City. We were staying downtown with Susan, in one of those Lower East Side neighborhoods that never sleep and where the streets are populated by people much of middle America would consider outside: street people, homeless people, winos, punks, bikers, people on drugs of one kind or another. They live among the neighborhood's less transient mainstays: Puerto Rican and eastern European families, old people, welfare recipients, people who are much more inside to more of the population.

Uptown, when we would venture "above 14th Street" to a museum or film, we moved among the New York business crowd, the uniformed or elegantly dressed hurrying from office to commuter train, the shoppers, the America at which much of this country's commercial advertising is aimed. They would certainly be considered inside by middle America, although among them I for one feel more outside than I do among the Lower East Side crowd (although in many ways I also feel outside among them).

And I guess that's the point: fitting comfortably into neither category, we were outsiders to both. And that got us to thinking about how much more of an outsider a person feels if she cannot identify or move within a group; and how much more insider she feels if she does, even when the group itself (as in the case of the homeless, the young punks, etc.) is so very outside.

In important ways, I think this is my problem at a place like Trinity College. I am neither an Etheridge Knight (Black ex-prisoner turned poet who is who he is, comes from a background and experience that necessitates his simply projecting his identity to the world and letting the chips fall where they may) nor an Annette Kolodny (highly formally educated academic with all the best credentials, employed with tenure at a good school).

I have purposefully chosen as illustrative of what I'm saying two people who are not ordinary in their respective milieus. Etheridge for obvious reasons; and Annette because she challenged the U.S. university system in a situation of blatant sex discrimination, battled the University of New Hampshire for close to five years in a law suit, suffered all manner of indignities and finally won a seven figure settlement. Both of these people sometimes or constantly move in academic circles, neither is totally a part of them, but both are very definitely from a specific place of his/her own, and insider to that place.

I often seem to be from neither side and at the same time from both, a traveler along our Möbius strip. With my white, middle-class origin, I have had access to the type of culture that enables me to cross certain lines. My ideas, my experience in Latin America, my commitments, and of course most obviously my current political situation set me apart. I am neither entirely one nor the other, and so I must work harder than most to protect my own insiderness (which is precisely what the government is trying to disrupt or destroy). This explains why I sometimes feel like such an outsider on the Trinity campus, a place where socially-conditioned insiderness is so highly cultivated and rewarded. The longer I work here, the better I am able to move within this situation. But I am always conscious of my difference.

In fact, in whatever new situation, every time I am introduced to someone I have not seen before, every time I appear at even the most ordinary of social functions, every single handshake or smile, carries with it the knowledge that, more likely than not, I must somehow cut through the antagonism, fear, curiosity or discomfort which now somehow goes along with perfectly simple encounters. Some days it's depressing; some days only exhausting.

When I am attacked on a call-in talk show by the most virulent of conservatives, branded with every offensive name there is, and told to "go back where I came from(!)," I still feel very much myself, inside. If I am appreciated, applauded, praised (like dropping by at the local Hartford bookstore the other night, and noticing that a large portion of their September events flyer was devoted to welcoming me to the city!), I also feel inside.

It is the murkiness and ambivalence of the in-between state that makes me feel most outside: outside in terms of general socially-acknowledged categories—and outside the type of concrete honest interaction which provides the reality-check apparently necessary to convince me that I am indeed who I am, insider to myself.

The uncertainty about the move east, with all its various corners and cracks, has heightened this neither/nor quality in my life. I've written a short sequence of poems I know comes out of this experience:

Bleak September

When Margaret entered the room
homeowners stretched through doorways
upstairs into further clusters
where conversations emptied, refilled,
faces circling mouths, eyes following a piper's dream
of neckties, the music of glasses, zoom-lensed
into *how good to see you my dear* and out again,
no time to wait for answers.

In this place in this September bleakness
one, a guest like myself,
might have turned,
might have followed her slight limp
momentarily carved a silent place among the olives
or stood aside
for the South African miner holding her tired arm.
Man or woman. But no one did.

No one missed a chance
in perfect conversation, center
of hollowed gravity.
No one skipped an offer of morsels
offered by working people, laughter, home products
with some meteor world as future.

No one stopped smiling, no one noticed
how the effervescence in their glasses turned to blood.

The miner raised and lowered his body into dance.
Bleak September pulled us toward October's sound.

Brian's Legs

*In September 1987 at the Concord, California Navy weapons
station, a Vietnam veteran named S. Brian Willson placed his
body on the track to protest a munitions train carrying
weaponry for the contras in Nicaragua. The train's engineer
had orders not to stop.*

In Margaret's chest Brian's body
resists the image of a train
following orders fast along a track.
Brian's train
is orders all the way
down years and thundering of track
orders to carry death to issue death
to anyone saying no against its charge.

Brian's body survived Vietnam, survived
 its orders in Vietnam
its hunger on the Capitol steps.
Brian's mind changed rhythms
through jungles and granite, Brian's legs went
not in a distant memory of war
but here at home
beneath a train with blood on its wheels.

Brian's legs
as in no I will not go,
I will not send loss to mothers,
grim lead to peasant children.
Brian's torn legs
surviving in my chest.

First Footnote

When Margaret writes her own name Margaret
into a poem
readers must stop and consider the evidence.
Who has gone home from work
on this particular Friday night. Who
walks along one side of a river
knowing what lies in wait on the other side
and walks still, following with her longest beam
the object of her search.
Who has taken your hand when you did not even know
you were holding it out.
Who is this woman who weaves her own name
into the fabric of her words?

This woman, Margaret, no longer looks for a place to hide.
She hides, yes, in those parts of her body
where doors have opened.
But she looks for a place, a safe place, to stand
before her altar in this life.

Second Footnote

They drag me away. I watch them
walking off, hauling my thrashing body,
watch as my starts of resistance
diminish against their dull dragging gait.
I have nothing left but my voice.
With it
I say Margaret Margaret Margaret Margaret
until they drop me and run
discarding me as they go.
I laugh.
I have myself back again. I am home.

Perhaps, in using my own name over and over again (something I have rarely done in my poetry), I am attempting to put myself back into a life from which I sometimes feel I am absent.

Something you say in one of your letters ties in with something Barbara has recently mentioned, out of her childhood in a fundamentalist family. She talks about how she—and so many others—were taught that all good comes from outside (God) while all bad comes from within (temptation, sin). Good is therefore attained by obedience to Him (interpreted, in her family, by the very rigid norms imposed by fundamentalism); bad will be the result of following your feelings, questioning, moving out, rejecting that world view.

Naturally this leads to a sense of self in which insider and outsider concepts are reversed. You grow up unable to trust yourself (because all that comes from you must be bad) and only being able to believe in some fabricated and rigid authority from which all good is promised.

To me this is a particularly terrifying picture. When I look at the Contragate hearings, or some other image out of the life of this administration, it seems very much in line with the above reversal. What is projected as good, is really bad. What is projected as honest, is a lie. All we have to do is make the initial reversal and we're in tune with so-called reality. More and more it seems to me that living comfortably in this country depends upon being able almost unconsciously to make this type of reversal.

Someone recently made the comment that the general public accepts an actor or actress playing the role of a particular public figure more readily than they can accept the public figure. The actor takes the place of the real person. A friend who teaches here at Trinity spoke of a student who admitted to not knowing there were Black doctors in this country until he began watching Cosby on television! The actor is so much easier to grasp and understand. Acknowledging the existence of the real person, dealing with that existence, makes demands that threaten complacency. Of course in Reagan, as actor-president, we have it both ways.

Much love,

Margaret

154

Letter Fourteen

Woods Hole, Massachusetts
September 12th, 1987

Dearest Margaret:

I have never thought through, much less written about, the development of my sexuality but clearly it has many insider/outsider dimensions. Now I want to write you about it and, as always, I'll begin at the beginning.

I grew up in a sexually "enlightened" household. That means that I found out that little girls and boys look different before I was four, when my brother was born. I remember the incident. I and a little boy were playing in a friend's garden and either were naked or, more likely, he had to pee and in European fashion, his mother simply pulled him slightly aside to do it. I found it very interesting, but was old enough not to comment until my mother and I were alone, when I asked her what his problem was. (I knew about "cripples" since Vienna was full of World War I veterans minus limbs or otherwise deformed—most of them beggars, so that I thought for a while that anyone with a physical disability was a beggar and once tried to give money to a man in a wheel chair who gently, but firmly, refused, much to my embarrassment.) People whose bodies were different from mine were outsiders to me, however mildly. My mother told me that all boys had a penis and used it to pee.

When my mother was pregnant she told me that she had a baby inside her. I think I assumed it got there by her eating something. I wanted a sister, not a brother, but don't know whether it had to do with penises or other impressions I had got of boys. There was a cobbled embankment outside our apartment windows and boys used to slide down it. It looked like fun and I wanted to try, too, but our maid told me it wasn't a good thing to do because it tears your pants. So, I told people I didn't want a brother because boys tear their pants, but I may have had other, more profound, reasons.

I don't know when I first heard how babies are made, but am pretty sure my father was the one who told me. He was less reserved than my mother and had an easier time talking about these things. He also used foul language casually, a Viennese habit and something my mother didn't like and never did. He must have walked around the house naked, whereas my mother didn't. I distinctly remember the first time I saw a woman naked (changing into a bathing suit) and how amazed I was at how different she looked from me, with all that axillary and pubic hair and those breasts. I must have seen my mother's breasts when she nursed my brother, but may have associated them with nursing the same way her distended body went with being pregnant. I don't remember the first time I saw a man naked. So, I assume I grew up seeing my father naked (which would be in character), but not my mother (also in character).

Once my brother was born, I saw him naked all the time because we shared sleeping quarters until we left Vienna, when he was ten and I, fourteen. I remember touching his penis in a giggly sort of way, but don't recall his touching my vulva. The only person who touched me there, other than to wash me, was a friend at the Gymnasium. We used to masturbate each other under our desks during class. She enjoyed it, but I thought it tickled too much. When I told my mother about it, she said we shouldn't do it because we'd get into a lot of trouble if someone saw us. I reported that to my friend, who was horrified that I had spoken to my mother and we stopped.

When I say that my father told me where babies come from, it was the usual pseudo-explanation that even enlightened parents give their children—about penises, vaginas, eggs, and sperm, but nothing about sexuality and pleasure. For a long time I assumed that my parents only had sex when they wanted children and was much put out when I learned that I was a mere by-product of something they did for their own enjoyment. I was eleven or twelve at the time and the thought must have occurred to me that some day I'd want to do it, too. But I went to a girls' school and knew few boys other than my brother and my grown-up cousins, who already had girl friends or fiancées. I speculated whether I'd marry one of the two or three boys I knew after we grew up, but didn't give it much thought. All my strong friendships were with girls and the first stirrings of erotic love were towards women teachers. Several of us were "in love" with the more friendly teachers (some of our teachers were real horrors!) and used to compare notes about the amount of attention each of us could garner. The teachers no doubt knew what was up and waited for it to pass, which it did.

At that point I had no idea that there was a possibility of sexual love between people of the same sex, but that didn't trouble me and in fact didn't register. I must have assumed that it was okay for girls to be in love with women and that when I got to be a woman I'd love a man, since that's what women did. None of this seemed out of the ordinary and none of it made me feel different or outsider, because lots of us girls were having similar experiences. I felt sufficiently at ease with my parents that whenever I had questions I would ask (as with my experience of mutual masturbation) and my parents were enlightened enough not to make a big deal of it.

In an Austrian all-girls school, we did not experience the erotic and sexual pressures that girls of that age did (and still do) in the United States. I began to want fancy shoes with heels as well as silk stockings, but that's as far as it went. No make-up. (My mother didn't wear any.) No dates. There was the thought that I might go to dancing class (ballroom, that is) "next year," but Hitler intervened and I went to Boston, instead. There I found myself among adolescents who had boys and clothes and dates very much on their minds and I opted out of that in the way I've described earlier. I became an outsider to the whole scene, with no special accent on the sexual part.

I didn't go on dates until I came to Radcliffe at seventeen. Of course, I knew boys from school and we'd go out in groups, but I did not participate in the dating scene. What's more, partly from what I had taken in about sexual mores in Vienna, partly on the basis of what I worked out myself, I was disgusted by the standard American sexual and dating mores—the ascending scale of holding hands, kissing, petting, "going the limit," "going all the way." As far as I was concerned, you either wanted to have sex with someone or you didn't. If you did, you "went all the way"; if you didn't, you didn't take part in any of it. I refused to recognize a distinction between sexual kissing and sexual intercourse. So, I was an outsider to the accepted mores, but felt comfortable with my own feelings on the subject and assumed they were Viennese, although I don't know to this day whether they were. Since I was an outsider to the entire scene, anyway, being an outsider to this part of it didn't increase my alienation to a significant degree.

My first serious feelings of erotic love were toward a woman counselor at a summer camp I went to when I was sixteen. I was troubled by it because I couldn't figure out what to do with my feelings. She was very much involved with a man (a married man, at that, with a wife and children at the same camp). Since she was the music counselor and I played the piano, I had no problem spending time with her and getting her attention, but of course no sexual contact. And I didn't expect any because I knew that's what happens between women and men, not between women.

I stayed in love with her for about half a year and just felt sad that there was no possibility of bringing it to any sort of fruition. I don't think I was still inclined to talk with my mother about those sorts of things, but if I did, she probably said something consoling like "you'll get over it" without giving "it" a name.

No doubt, she would have been reluctant to give it the appropriate name, a word I didn't hear until that summer in Vermont before I went to college. There I discovered that Oscar Wilde looked the way he did on purpose, that he was homosexual, that there is such a thing and that there are Lesbians. Incidentally, I don't think the five of us in Vermont asked ourselves whether we were Lesbians, although there was a lot of borderline sexuality. For example, we slept naked, two to a bed. But we talked about sexuality only in terms of men even though the other four had encountered homosexuality in New York, female and male.

Ruth's high school yearbook picture, Brookline, 1941

As I told you before, by the time I came to college, I had decided to turn over a new leaf and fit in better. I went to freshman dances, tried to get to know Harvard men, shortly met Frank

Hubbard and other Harvard students, and became "normal." Did I feel insider? No. I fell in with other outsiders, including Frank, who was fighting his battles with his conventional mother. At that point I also had someone I called my boyfriend in New York, a boy I had known from Vienna, the brother of one of the girls in Vermont. (Until this moment, I had forgotten about him.) We saw each other on rare visits when we held hands and kissed. That was because he was not prepared to do more, not I. My all-or-nothing principles stood, but what could I do? Sometime during my freshman year I went to bed with Frank, a first for both of us and pretty experimental and unsatisfactory. We married during my sophomore year and, as you know, stayed married for about eight years, but our sexual relationship never amounted to much.

During those years I had a number of lovers, all of them male. Many of these encounters were experiments in human relationships more than experiences with sex or love. I met my first bona fide Lesbian in college, a woman who was very mixed up about her sexuality and place in the world (as well she might be at that time). Two of her women lovers had been kicked out of college for being Lesbians, while she had not, and of course this made her feel guilty. Shortly after that trauma, she had married a graduate student whom she felt she was torturing with her dissatisfactions and problems. She made an emotional, though not physical, pass at me, and I fled. After that we continued as cool and distant acquaintances.

From then on, I was keenly aware of gays (mostly men), sometimes wondered whether I was Lesbian because I didn't fit most of the accepted female stereotypes, and talked about it with Frank. But that's as far as it went. I fell in love with George when I was twenty, and have written you about that. What's interesting is that I have not been as much in love with anyone else, although I have had other lovers. I think an important reason I let myself get that deeply involved with George (and perhaps he with me) was that for a long time both of us took it for granted that because of our other commitments, it was impossible for us to have a profound, long-lasting relationship. Therefore neither of us had our guard up. I certainly didn't and let myself get more involved than I have with anyone else, male or female. Does that mean that I have always kept part of myself outside all my sexual relationships? Perhaps. And I certainly have kept the sexual me outside my relationships with women.

I was very homophobic all through the 1950s and 1960s. Mostly toward men, because I didn't know any Lesbians, or rather, didn't know I did. Later, around 1972, when one of my closest friends, who I knew was having a very troubled love affair, finally "confessed" that it was with a woman, I was surprised but not shocked or put off. In fact, before she told me that she was a Lesbian, I once suggested that we, or she, should be more open to the possibility of Lesbian relationships (not said as a come-on). She responded that she had tried, but that it hadn't helped her out of her troubles. I guess my involvement with feminism and women, which began in the late sixties, did away with my overt homophobia. Internalized homophobia I may still have, as all of us do who grow up in a homophobic society.

I told my children that this friend, whom they knew well, was a Lesbian when she entered into a new relationship and started coming to our house with her lover. So, they both were familiar with the reality (not just the idea) before or early in their adolescence. Later, at the public high school they attended, students were experimenting with all kinds of sexuality and several of their friends came out as gay or bisexual before they graduated. (Interestingly, neither Elijah nor Debbie had their first sexual experiences in high school, despite the volume and variety of it there. I don't know what that means except that they, like me, don't seem to mind staying outside the accepted mores.)

As far as I know, to date all Elijah's sexual experiences have been with women. Debbie's first was with a man, her second and long-lasting one, with Brooke, a woman. She has said that both times, she fell in love with a person, not a gender, although now she, of course, identifies as a Lesbian. In a homophobic society, being a Lesbian obviously has all sorts of meanings it would not have if the gender of one's lover were irrelevant. For one thing, the world does not give the same weight to Lesbian and heterosexual relationships. Even most people who supposedly acknowledge a love relationship between two women, do not take it as seriously and give it the kind of respect they give to heterosexual relationships. Debbie, Brooke and I have noticed this when we have traveled together. If Debbie's lover were a man, the world would treat us as Debbie-and-her-lover plus me, her mother. Since Brooke is a woman, we are Debbie-and-her-mother (or I-and-my-daughter) plus Debbie's (or our) friend. And nothing we do, short of shaking people (which one doesn't usually do with strangers or casual acquaintances) changes that.

In the same way, I may "feel" Lesbian in the depth of my identification with women, but I am not. The world takes my relationship to my partner ever so much more seriously than it would if she were a woman, no matter how long the relationship lasts and how much it means to the two of us.

From the insider/outsider perspective, I believe that although my sexual relationships have all been with men, I have felt and still feel an outsider to the sexual and social mores and definitions of what proper heterosexual relationships should look like. In my relationship with Frank, I was the scientist and bread-winner, while he was the literary person and, later, craftsman/artist. I worked all hours at the lab, he was at home a lot more than I, etc. In my relationship with George, we were closeted for many years and

Ruth and George, Woods Hole, 1983

when we "came out" it was an unconventional relationship because of our previous marital histories (which were more unusual then than now), the difference in our ages, the fact that there was no thought that I'd stop being a scientist and become a "wife," that I shortly became a feminist and we had to change our relationship in many ways, that both of us stopped doing science and started living much more separate and independent lives, and so on. Our relationships with our children also have been somewhat unconventional and closer than customary.

So, although I have nominally been an insider, in the sense of living with a man, except when I've lived alone, I don't feel like an insider sexually, either. I am one when I fill out official forms, but not when I am living my life. Yet I cannot identify as Lesbian because of my feelings about women, as long as the world grants me heterosexual privilege, just as I cannot be completely iden-tified with the Black struggle because my skin is white. The world treats us according to indicators that may not be all that significant to us personally, but if we live with men and/or our skin is white, that shields us from racist and/or homophobic attacks. And since my relationship with George and my children (in other words, my family) is what grounds me and lets me be at one with myself, I can express solidarity with my Lesbian sisters and join their struggles, but cannot complain if they treat me as an outsider some of the time.

Meanwhile Debbie and Brooke have moved to San Francisco so they can stop being noticed and be, to use their words, "ordinary, normal, and boring." I know what they mean, but sure wish they could be boring nearer to where I live.

This seems like a good place to stop.

Much love,

Ruth

Letter Fifteen

Hartford, Connecticut
September 22nd, 1987

Dearest Ruth:

Your last letter sparked so many thoughts and ponderings about my own sexuality, what forces lead us in different directions, how contrived is so much of society's message regarding the "appropriate" or "inappropriate" ways of expressing ourselves sexually, and how those socially-imposed assumptions and signals may affect the way we are in other areas of life. Looking back, I think I have always felt outside, in terms of my sexuality.

Although I have few and disjointed memories of childhood sexual feelings—and my recent discovery of the incest experience probably explains why—I do know that even as an adolescent I felt like an outsider in this respect.

Your all-or-nothing philosophy when you came to this country from Vienna was especially interesting to me. It holds so much more inner integrity than the socially-conditioned mores, in terms of being in touch with one's body, and owning it. A typical product of my time (late forties to mid and late fifties) and place (Albuquerque, a provincial American city in the west), I was agonizingly caught up in the contradictions. My body often felt engaged in secret war with the accepted conventions.

During my teens, in my class, generation, and cultural milieu, there were very definitely "good" girls and "bad" girls. The good girls saved "it" for marriage, and at each stage of the game (and a game it surely was!) we were expected to provide service to a specified point relevant to the situation at hand. That is, we kissed on the lips on perhaps a third or fourth date, if the boy in question complied with the expected male behavior. If we were going steady we could neck (generally meaning kissing and hugging and rubbing up against one another, but without much serious below-the-neck activity).

Petting was a good deal more serious, and involved letting the boy fondle our breasts and other less clearly specified parts of our bodies. It was reserved for girls who had acknowledged, long-standing relationships. These were serious social norms, and observing them had a good deal more to do with being inside or out than most other criteria by which a person's worth might be measured. We learned early that appearances were what counted, what others thought of us was more important than what we felt, what we needed, or what we thought of ourselves.

The only type of sexuality ever considered, of course, was male/female; homosexuality was never mentioned—except in faint whispers or barely accessible books we read while baby-sitting some neighbor's child. It had nothing to do with us. (I had a Lesbian aunt who lived with her life-long companion, and both were close to my parents. They are long dead, and to this day when I refer to them as Lesbians my parents, exceptionally open-minded as they are, will say "Well, we don't really *know* that.")

I never seemed to be in tune with the sexual norms of my youth. I don't think I know anyone who was. As the years go by and I watch my own children grow and develop, I am more and more convinced that the patriarchy in a capitalist commodity-oriented society literally programs a culture in which our vital human needs are subservient to the system's priorities: the extreme competitiveness that is a product of free enterprise, ever increasing profit, ways of looking at the world and at the self which avoid addressing issues of substance. For many this programming means a total distortion of her or his sexual identity; of other aspects of the identity too. At the very least, there are the years lost in that useless search for ease while one is forced into so many uneasy roles.

In high school I began dating boys who were as shy and frightened as I was. I retain vivid images of Tommy whose voice was barely audible when he called to ask what color dress I would be wearing to the prom, Dave whose lips were an impenetrable barrier when he finally kissed me on our twentieth date, Larry whose reserve I understood years later when he told me he was gay, Sam for whom dating meant endless philosophical discussions concerning the existence of God (he became a Baptist preacher).

Less frequent, but certainly also a part of my introduction to sexuality, were the occasional dates with boys who ignored the good girl/bad girl game completely. One, whose name I can no longer remember, repeatedly forced and twisted his tongue into my mouth, stopping only long enough to talk about bayonets and other implements of war! I was too scared to do anything but go along with his demands. Another, whose name I *do* remember (it was Freddy, and he was All-State in football) tried to rape me in the mountain foothills I now call home. I was insider to myself enough by that time to struggle, free myself, and run.

I had my first "complete" sexual experience with a man (more a boy than a man) when I was seventeen. As with your first experience of this kind, it eventually led to marriage. And I am sure the decision to marry him was based, along with simply wanting to get off on my own (and not imagining another way to do that), on the fact that I had "lost my virginity" to him.

That was a four-year marriage, unhappy on many counts, and sexually extremely unhappy. No amount of reading in the sex manuals of the times, no amount of advice-seeking from those I considered older and wiser than myself, not even the visits to a psychiatrist which were my final recourse, allowed me to look to myself and my own needs in an effort to find a way out. I eventually did find a way out, though. For my survival I had to.

My parents, as I've said, were exceptionally understanding and open about sexuality, and had I not been so very influenced by peer pressure and the social mores of the times, I might have saved myself some real misery by listening to them. Like most other young people, I had to find things out in my own way.

After my first marriage and divorce, I entered a period of pretty frenetic sexual activity; some would call it promiscuity. In lower Manhattan I moved among a group of artists and writers whose philosophy about sex was that it was something to be taken lightly: one satisfied needs, did what felt good (feelings, of course, deeply influenced by what one had grown up believing was acceptable), and didn't worry too much about formalities. (This was pre-herpes, pre-AIDS America; even the traditional sexually transmitted diseases were not very prevalent among the artists.)

Most people were not married. They lived together for varying periods of time. Or didn't. Independence was loudly touted—for women as well as men—but women were definitely expected, by everyone, to play subservient roles in all areas of interaction.

Looking back, it has always seemed to me that we women among the artists and writers of those times were the original groupies. We had our work, it was important to us, our lives were certainly not defined by camp-follower conduct; but we frequented the men, tried to write or paint like the men, and wanted to be accepted by the men. In the art world many people were gay, of course, and that was acknowledged—but in my particular territory they were definitely other, definitely outside.

I had relationships; encounters might more accurately describe most of them. Some lasted months. Some only weeks or days. A few were serious. Many were so short that I can no longer remember names, or even faces. I talked myself into the idea that this was a good alternative lifestyle. Bourgeois marriage, along with other state institutions, was clearly a hypocritical establishment. This was all so much easier. We never talked about our loneliness.

But I certainly felt lonely. And that was critical, I believe, in my decision in 1959 to have a child. I didn't want another marriage, certainly not like the one I had already endured. But I wanted a child, and I saw no reason why I shouldn't have one. I made deliberate plans to get pregnant (which had nothing at all to do with sexuality, but a great deal to do with wanting to be a mother); and I chose a man I respected as a human being, whose genes seemed good, who was not a user of hard drugs, or otherwise crazy. Of course I could not tell the man with whom I was having sex of my intention; that would not have been at all acceptable, even within our countercultural world.

Having Gregory, in October of 1960, was an important milestone for me. Sexual considerations were not paramount, but I think becoming a mother changed my sexual self-image in some fundamental sense. I was no longer alone, and having a child proved essential in my taking myself and my needs seriously in a long-range way. These are things I have only come to see much much later, of course, but I never again had an "affair" with only the moment in mind. Gregory was a part of my life; he had to be considered. When he was ten months old, I felt sexually as well as in many other ways fed up with New York. Together we moved to Mexico.

The loneliness was much more significant than I had allowed myself to believe. Companionship, a colleague, a friend: these were things I wanted in an intimate relationship, and the Bohemian veneer which so coated everything in New York made it seem difficult if not impossible to find those things there. In Mexico it might be easier. And indeed in some ways, it was.

I came to Mexico a young North American woman with a small child. Among Mexican artists and writers my connection with the New York art world was romanticized—and also feared. Sergio Mondragon, the Mexican poet I eventually married, was attracted to that vibrant free young woman, and just as determined to make (break) her into an acceptable and non-threatening Mexican bride.

We were married. We had two more children, Sarah and Ximena. We founded and edited a bilingual literary publication, *El Corno Emplumado/The Plumed Horn*, and in important ways became such a cultural institution that our differences were at first lost in the excitement of creating and connecting.

Sergio was really a very traditional Latin American male, with all the insecurities, fierce jealousies, and perversities of vision that implies. Sexually, we were never very well matched. In retrospect, I can see that he offered me the home, the security, the companionship, the stimulation of shared interests so lacking in most of my relationships to that point.

I retain memories that make me shudder in the telling. Once, in a restaurant, he imagined I was staring at some men at a nearby table. A violent scene followed. Much later, the fact that I received a close male friend of ours dressed only in a bathrobe (that buttoned to my chin, had long sleeves, and fell full-length to the floor) provoked his not speaking to me for a week. After eight years—and of course a distancing in many areas, including the political—I left Sergio. But not before he had shouted at me: "Look at you, a divorced woman with three children! Who do you think will want you now?"

And make no mistake, this was very much about sexuality. To be wanted, that was your basic female sexual identity. And we women were conditioned to internalize that as much as the men. The supreme objectification: you were either wanted or discarded, used and/or abused, taken or rejected, or all of the above. And depending on which of these things you were, you were either inside or out.

After the relationship with Sergio I had a few others, eventually living with Robert Cohen for another seven or eight years—and having my fourth child, Ana, with him.

My interest here is not to rewrite that earlier letter in which I trace my personal history. It's not even to list particular relationships, particular men, but to attempt to trace, somehow, my feelings about my own sexual identity, and to what extent those feelings, as they developed and changed, placed me in an insider or outsider position vis-à-vis society, and myself.

Robert and I moved to Cuba in very stressful circumstances; I had been forced into hiding as a result of political repression in Mexico. It was 1969.

The most recent wave of feminism had just broken along the underbelly of some of the industrialized societies—most notably the United States, France, and England—and news of ideas and events began filtering into the so-called Third World. I had begun collecting material from the U.S. women's movement late in 1968, and while still in Mexico published what would become the first anthology of those pieces in Spanish. In Cuba I was curious about what socialism meant for women. My first full-time project there was a two-year study of oral histories which became my first book on Cuban women, *Cuban Women Now.**

There's no doubt about it. As with you, my encounter with the feminist movement, my realization that the problems I had faced apparently so alone were shared by thousands, millions of women everywhere; this was essential in my re-evaluation of my own sexuality.

I could now articulate feelings of inequality and supposed inadequacy and identify them as social ills, not simply my problems, my fault. In my relationship with Robert we struggled hard around issues of household roles, childcare, independence. In fact, like many other couples of those years, we grew a great deal as individuals, but struggled ourselves right out of the relationship.

In Cuba I had a sexual experience that would affect me deeply. I was working on the book about Cuban women, traveling around the country with a couple of assistants, and one night, in a rain-battered hotel room in the eastern city of Bayamo, woke to find one of my (female) co-workers sexually assaulting me. I could now add this attempted rape by a woman to the attempted rape by a man so many years before—and the woman's assault, coming as it did from a co-worker and close friend, proved much the more painful. You know, Ruth, my asthma dates from that night.

But, as I say, feminism came into my life with power and relief. I bonded with women in ways I had rarely been able to do with men. These were not sexual bondings. Nonetheless my relationships with women friends became fundamental—and ongoing in ways that relationships with my male lovers almost never did. I often wondered why I felt such a dichotomy in my way of relating to men and women; I chose men as lovers (if conditioning can be called choice), but I really *loved* a number of women. My intimate relationships with men lasted five, six, eight years maximum. I have several important friendships with women that go back fifteen, twenty, even thirty years.

Trying to respond to that back then, I simply assumed that I was as close to the socially-accepted norm as possible. I had not been conditioned to question that assumption. Few are, in this

* *Cuban Women Now* by Margaret Randall. Toronto, Canada: Women's Press, 1974.

society. Looking back, I'm sure age, background, and—very specifically—place, had a great deal to do with the fact that I developed these deep relationships with women but continued to relate sexually only to men.

We were in Latin America, and we lived in the fast-changing sociopolitical upheavals of countries like Cuba, and later

Margaret cutting cane in Cuba, 1970

171

Nicaragua, where you didn't worry too much about your sexuality. You didn't worry too much about your personal life at any level. There was far too much to be done in the area of communal struggle. The women's movements were also quite different in those countries, and the gay movement had not developed in them as it had in the United States.

After Robert and I split up, I lived for five years with a Colombian poet. Then I was essentially alone for four years until I fell in love with Floyce—and returned to the United States. In all of these relationships, with all of these quite different men, I felt sexually outside—of the men, society, and myself. I am not only, or even principally, speaking about physical sexuality; I am speaking about gender issues: dependence and independence, power, control, freedom.

Oh, I was insider in that I fulfilled the expected norms, I was the female part of a heterosexual couple, and I acquired my quota of social authenticity and privilege because of it. Often the sex felt good. I also shared some very real and beautiful things with these men. But I remained outside—of the couple, and ultimately of myself—because I was never really comfortable. I always felt like a misfit. I remember sometimes feeling literally invaded. And I invented ways in which I could, at least for a while, change my understanding of what I wanted in order to seem more insider to myself.

The choices I saw were those of coupling with a man—in any one of the more or less acceptable variants—or living alone. This latter choice, unthinkable as it seemed when I was growing up (the labels for it were clear enough: spinster, old maid, woman who couldn't get a man), did seem more acceptable when I was in my thirties and forties. And I tried periods of that. But the need for another kind of companionship was always there; children and friends were rarely enough.

When I visited the United States in 1983, I entered a love relationship with Floyce. When I returned to stay, we began living together and were married in February of 1984.

At the same time, I came home to the community of women which had long been such an important part of my life. This is a community that crosses national and cultural boundaries of

172

course, but out of deeply shared roots there is a particular sisterhood with North American women—whose backgrounds, traditions, and concerns have paralleled my own—that made coming home to *this* community of women an especially profound experience.

I find myself deeply disturbed by the media, by the blanket heterosexist image of society which assumes that Lesbians are outside (worse yet, invisible). I am sure I am even more aware of this than many Lesbians and gay men who have been out most of their lives but do not necessarily have a feminist consciousness—because I have long made it a point to study the media with regard to its distortion of class, race, and gender.

On the other side of this anger at heterosexist assumptions is a world of culture, traditions, art, language, poetry, that constitutes a Lesbian heritage—lost to us all until our women's movement began to unearth it in recent years. As a latecomer to these questions and as a person who delights in cultural diversity, I am excited when I come across pieces of this part of our lost history. This is an experience that always pulls me inside.

I continue to love some of the men with whom I have lived, I continue to feel strong bonds with all those who have been important in my life. But I now understand an important measure of my long discomfort, my condition as misfit, my unease, my outsiderness. The years of gradually coming to understand that things were not as they had been advertised, and seeking—with alternate desperation or resignation—the reasons for that. The years of pretending, of making do, of making concessions, of looking elsewhere for one whole piece of my identity. The struggle of those years has come home to roost or nest, as it were. It is a profoundly insider experience.

Much love,

Margaret

Letter Sixteen

Dearest Ruth:

I'm tremendously interested in this business of getting strength from knowing that one is outside. Maybe because of my current situation with INS. I guess I have always gotten a certain amount of strength from identifying with the outsider pole, primarily because I've had a great need to act in accordance with my ideals: politically, spiritually, humanly. This seems necessary for my identity.

Here again I think the tension itself is important. And I know how forces that are consistently superior—in resources, in strength, in authority—can gradually erode bits and pieces of our own strength, so that we become physically unable to represent our chosen stance. The choice may still be there, the desire to be faithful to it as well, but living day-in day-out with the presence of certain threats—to our physical integrity and health, to our wholeness, energies, creativity, peace of mind, to the people we love—can tear at our personhood, at our capacity to create an inside for ourselves, even within our most deeply-held beliefs.

Recent (as well as ancient) history is full of examples of this. People forced into hiding for long periods of time. People confined in prisons for years. People enduring physical and psychological torture. And on other levels, people who grow up in a context of ongoing class, race, or gender oppression. Working people who are coerced into an upward mobility that blots out class consciousness. Blacks whose image of what they are is definitively altered by a white racist society. Women who accept domestic violence and who draw on it to internalize a sense of worthlessness. Gays and Lesbians who buy into the discrimination against them. All of us, simply by virtue of being saturated with the media messages about who we are and what we need.

We have lots of examples of men and women—and even children—who have been battered beyond belief, people who have been tortured, whose families have been disappeared, who have suffered incredible psychological and physical devastation; and yet their capacity for forging an insider self-knowledge and dignity within the hell imposed upon them has allowed them to come through, with at least a part of their humanity in tact. (You referred to this in your first letter.)

We also know that situations such as these are capable of definitively warping the positive insider/outsider tension, invalidating it as motor and casting the victim (for such a person has truly become a victim) forever on the outsider side of the axis.

Forever is a big word. What about homeless people? What about the great masses of homeless, as contrasted, say, with the Bowery bums of my early New York years, men and a few women who were seen as anomalies within the social construct, not a growing class or caste? And what about people with AIDS? I'm not comparing people with AIDS to the homeless, here, for their situations are certainly different. But both are relatively recently-formed groups for which hope (or the lack of it) must be radically different from what it usually is. It would be interesting, and useful, to hear from some of these people about what their insider/outsider issues are.

I've been wanting to examine race in this context. Race and/or ethnicity. How does it place us inside or out? And what do we do with that? My own experience is not very dramatic. Still, it bears exploration.

My family background is Jewish. My father's family was of

175

German Jewish origin, and—socially, and to some extent religiously—they identified as Jews. My mother's family was part Jewish, part Protestant, and her parents from what I can tell did not present a clear identity in this respect. My maternal grandfather took up Christian Science, and became a practitioner (minister) of that faith. My mother was sent to a Quaker School as a child. I believe my father's family looked down on my mother's—I presume because they were not practicing Jews—and my father changed our surname shortly after I was born.

Where did this leave me? Well, I always had a vague sense of Jewishness, not generated by religious practice or even cultural attitudes, but it was there. How, why, I can't say. As a child I don't remember ever being taken to temple; I attended my first (and only) seder when I was in my forties. Perhaps it was the persecution of the Jews, certainly spoken of in my family, that somehow demanded I cast my lot with the oppressed. So, while I never embraced Judaism as a religion, and once a feminist found reasons to spurn Jewish religious tradition as I understand it, I passed along to my own children the knowledge that they had, in some profound way, Jewish history in their blood.

I remember my son Gregory, coming home in tears one day from his Mexican kindergarden because the teacher's Christmas story featured the Jews killing Christ. That night he dreamed the Jews had broken all the light bulbs in the house. Gregory was three or four at the time, but he clearly understood that a Jewish identity had something to do with him. I no longer remember how I gave him that consciousness.

Assimilation is a complex thing. You will be able to write about it more fully than I, because its contours have been more present in your life. Recently Susan Sherman and I have talked about some of the issues, attempting to articulate where we may fit, or not, on this map.

Today there is a reassessment on the part of many progressive Jewish people, among them many feminists; and their Jewishness as well as their need to rake through what has been made of it, are important in their understanding of cultural and religious roots. Perhaps all I can say, in terms of my own life, is that I don't have enough points of reference to claim more than an identification with the oppressed.

But I've long had a reproduction of that wonderful Lisa Kokin batique in which an Israeli and a Palestinian woman are facing one another and holding hands. The legend says something like: As Jews, our history of oppression allows us to understand the struggle of our Palestinian sisters and brothers. (The reproduction is back in New Mexico, so I'm just paraphrasing it here.) That batique and that legend are important to me; we need to bridge divisions, heal wounds—not make them deeper. I'm sure this would be a good place to address your question of several letters back, about how we can heal splits in the movement, between comrades, between all of us whose real interests should place us on the same side, not against one another. Only our common enemies benefit from the splits; "divide and conquer" is just another way of saying that if you keep us outside of our real inside, separated from our natural allies, you rob us of our greatest strength.

Ethnicity has inhabited my life in other ways. In Latin America I was a white woman — not just a woman of middle-class origins and from the United States, but a white woman, with all the outsider implications that fact projects in cultures where exploitation and oppression increase in direct proportion to the darkness of skin.

I've mentioned the Mexican woman whose baby I had just delivered verbalizing her desire that it be "white, like yours . . . " I had to fight through my whiteness, in Mexico and—although differently—also in Cuba and Nicaragua. And back in New Mexico after I taught a university course called Third World Women, I ended the semester convinced my skin was the wrong color to teach it again—at least in the North American southwest.

In New Mexico I remember a young woman student expressing her pain because she was of mixed heritage and felt accepted neither by Anglos nor Chicanos. Perhaps naively—at that point I had been home less than a year—I tried to get her to see that rather than half a heritage she had two. In a world less torn by racism, it could be true.

I had another student, once, a Black woman who has since

become one of my closest friends. In the first class she ever took from me, Women and Ethnicity, I asked the participants to do an impromptu oral history of their lives—one at the beginning of each week's meeting. This woman, who was then almost fifty, began by saying she had never really encountered racism in her life. And she went on to describe a life like that of any person of color in this country, rife with it. A couple of semesters later, this same woman credited myself and another professor with having opened her eyes, not only to the ways racism had affected her life but to the rich cultural and artistic heritage she had been aware of, but hadn't been able to consciously go to for strength. Having had a small part in giving that to my friend is one of the things I value in my life.

My own children frequently express the rootlessness and confusion that comes from an uncertain sense of place. And their problem, in some ways, is also an ethnic one. The two who are U.S. citizens know English only as a second language. In Latin America, where they grew up, they are too white: outside. But they are outside here, as well, by virtue of their language, their culture, and many of their points of reference and attitudes.

Because you and I, Ruth, have been able to make certain choices—which implies a degree of insiderness—our outsiderness has been a result of those choices rather than of an ongoing forced alienation. We have been able to keep the tension—and use it. Exceptions to this, as you point out, are your having come over as a Jewish immigrant from Austria, a refugee outside of language and custom; or my current situation with INS in which superior forces are (so far) threatening to rip me from family and place because of my ideas.

But even as an involuntary outsider, someone forced to become an immigrant, you still had choices. America was a land of opportunities for those of your class, color, and educational status. And I will have choices, too. If, at the end of my appeals, I lose my case, my class, intellectual condition, and network of supporters will enable me to choose another place to live. I will most probably not go hungry; I will most certainly not face torture or death. In this sense, we are still insiders in our outsiderness. We can take control of the tension that energizes our lives.

Of course there is always the matter of being so conditioned, internalizing oppression to such a degree, that we literally lose the capacity for choice. In our society choice is there, objectively speaking, for many more than realize it. This is why I continuously tell my students (most of whom have some choices, even if they do not know they do) that they must stop accepting the pseudo-options offered by the system as the only ones available and at least explore the possibility of other, more useful, ones. In many parts of the world, there really is no choice. Our analysis would be meaningless to an Ethiopian watching her children die of hunger, or to people in places where their only choice is between struggle or death, or maybe only between death and death.

(It occurs to me, here, that the threat of nuclear devastation presents the possibility, the first in history, of an area in which none of us has any control at all of the insider/outsider tension—perhaps this is one reason why the anti-nuclear movement is so strong; people are so desperate about making the least degree of progress, and the slightest change is seen as progress.)

When you talk about the issues that have split our movements, about what we can do to help us all to see that we need to be enlarging our outsider inside and struggling together because the forces against us are powerful and the danger imminent, I think of a lesson taught to me by a Vietnamese comrade during the war. And in some profound way this story brings more lucid ideological considerations to bear on the questions of race, class, gender.

In my memory I listen again to my Vietnamese friends in Havana explaining slowly and with great patience how important they felt it was to define one's circle of friends (comrades, colleagues, fellow- or sister-humans) as broadly as possible. You decide who the real enemy is, then work hard to bring everyone else into the vast circle that would do battle against that enemy. Then it's many against one. An easier victory. Once more you begin to draw your lines, set your boundaries, so that when a new enemy emerges you may do battle—from the position of greatest strength—with this new adversary. And on it goes, until of course you are all acceptably together, in a collective that has no trouble growing as one. Inside. It is a way of seeing humanity as truly more valuable than class, color, gender, or any other divisions; but without making concessions of principle around these important issues.

When I was much younger I saw myself as an outsider arrogantly inside in terms of my particular ideas, needs, direction. My best defense mechanism against the rigors of the larger society was simply keeping everyone else out. I didn't want them in. There was a certain defiant satisfaction, as you've said, in being almost alone in there, alone and proud.

As I've grown older, my insider circle has expanded, so that there are more and more different types of people in here with me. I no longer feel we all have to be available at all times or for the same kinds of exchange or sharing. Or that we must agree about any but matters of essential principle. We fulfill different needs with different people. And I know this is reciprocal; I fill some needs but certainly not all, for each of my friends.

Of course my political views have shaped me to a large extent, and I feel the threat of holocaust (of all kinds) so acutely that I work in every way I can so that we outsiders who are inside will increase in number and the self-proclaimed insiders who we know are outside, will lose their death-dealing power.

Much love,

Margaret

Letter Seventeen

Woods Hole, Massachusetts
October 1st, 1987

Dearest Margaret:

This is going to be a more difficult letter to write than usual because I want to explore some insider/outsider dimensions of being Jewish, something I tend to avoid thinking about. I'm not sure why; perhaps because it evokes painful associations with what happened when the Nazis took over Austria and I had to leave. I think, as usual, I would like to start with history, in this case with my grandparents.

All my grandparents were Jews and all were born in the eastern parts of the Austro-Hungarian empire, that became Czechoslovakia and Poland at the end of World War I. But I don't think any of them grew up in a shtetl. They were town or city folk.

My father's parents came to "the capital," Vienna, before any of their children were born and thought of themselves as Viennese when I knew them. They were religious in the sense that they lit sabbath candles, celebrated Passover, and observed the high holy days — Yom Kippur and Rosh Hashanah. My grandfather also was a functionary of some sort in his synagogue. But they did not keep a kosher household.

My mother's parents did not come to Vienna until after their children were of school age and always thought of themselves as Polish Jews. The story I have been told is that they moved to Vienna because my mother was talented in music and they wanted her to have better educational opportunities than she was likely to get in the "provinces." They observed the sabbath and the Jewish holidays and held to the Jewish dietary laws. Even after my grandmother came to live with us in the United States, she kept her own dishes— separate ones for meat and dairy and a separate set of both for Passover—and prepared her own food.

So, both my parents grew up in relatively observant, Jewish households, but both broke away. They did not take part in any Jewish rituals or holidays. My father was an atheist and my mother calls herself agnostic. To the dismay of my grandparents, my brother was not even circumcised, because my mother considered it an uncalled-for mutilation.

To avoid family controversies, my parents entered my brother and me into the rolls of the Viennese Jewish Community when we were born but until I went to school, I did not know anything about religion, Jews, Christians, or god. Austria, being a Catholic state with a state church, had compulsory religious instruction. So, when I was six, I discovered the concept of religion and that I was Jewish, whereas about half of my classmates were Catholic, and a few were Protestant. From first grade on we had two hours a week of religious instruction when our class was split up into Catholics and Jews. There were so few Protestants that they had to get their instruction elsewhere after school. At first, this introduced awkward barriers, but we soon got used to it and took little notice, though I think it encouraged us to form cliques along lines of religious denomination (which I suppose was part of the aim of the exercise).

My first encounter with religious instruction was traumatic because of my utter ignorance. The teacher assumed all of us were familiar with the routine religious observances, but I had not heard of any of them. My mother was urged to teach me the basic Jewish religious practices. So she sent me off to watch my grandparents light sabbath candles and break the ritual bread. I also participated in their seder and visited them in the synagogue on the high holy days. My only positive memory of that period is of drawing a lurid comic strip about the story of Cain and Abel.

Our religion teachers insisted we attend Saturday afternoon children's services at the synagogue and I did that occasionally. But religion did not play an important role in my life, except for a brief time, when I was about ten and began to worry that my parents would suffer for their irreligiousness after they died (a whiff of Catholicism, no doubt). For a while, I prayed every evening in an effort to redeem their sins, but soon gave up.

I want to be perfectly clear: I knew we were Jewish and by the time I was ten I also knew that anti-Semitism was rampant in neighboring Germany and widespread in Austria, although I had no personal contact with it. I did not feel that being Jewish made me an outsider in Austria, nor did I feel that not being religious made me an outsider among Jews. My parents had a large circle of friends, most of them Jews like us, who were not religious.

Zionism was a political issue while I was growing up. One of my mother's cousins, who often baby-sat for us, was studying Hebrew and eventually emigrated to Palestine; but that did not seem all that different from her sister, who studied English and emigrated to London. I knew that my father was opposed to Zionism because, as a socialist, he opposed all manifestations of nationalism.

I dwell on this history because it colors my present position, which is an outsider position among most American Jews and Jewish feminists. When I read *The Tribe of Dina** last year, which is a fine collection of diverse writings by Jewish feminists in the United States and Israel, much as the articles interested me, none reflected my own experience, which is the experience of a western European Jew, not of an eastern or sephardic one. The only things I have read that speak to me personally are the writings of Hannah Arendt. Both in her biography of Rahel Varnhagen, an assimilated Jewess who was important in Berlin society around 1800, and in her book on *The Origins of Totalitarianism,*** Arendt describes what

* *The Tribe of Dina: A Jewish Women's Anthology* edited by Melanie Kaye/Kantrowitz and Irena Klepfisz. Montpelier, VT: Sinister Wisdom Books, 1986.
** *Rahel Varnhagen, the Life of a Jewish Woman* by Hannah Arendt. New York: Harcourt Brace Jovanovich, 1974; and *The Origins of Totalitarianism: New Edition with Expanded Prefaces* by Hannah Arendt. New York: Harcourt Brace Jovanovich, 1979.

Jewish assimilation in western Europe was like and analyzes the resulting integration of Jewish and non-Jewish culture. Her discussion rings true to me. It is where I come from. Not from a Jewish culture, but from a Jewish-European one.

Many Jews who lived in western Europe (often for centuries) assimilated and thought of themselves as Germans, Danes, Dutch, and so forth. And their cultural contributions are part of what we mean by European culture. This has been true in politics, philosophy, literature, music, painting, sculpture, science, as well as in business. Think of Disraeli, Marx, Rosa Luxemburg, Heine, Kafka, Mendelssohn, Schönberg, Kokoschka, Freud, Reich, Einstein . . . Why go on making lists? Many of them retained their Jewish faith, others became non-believers or Christians. None produced the kind of *Jewish* culture we associate with eastern European or with sephardic Jews. Just compare Kafka and Isaac Bashevis Singer.

The continuous, active discrimination against Jews in Russia and Poland of course resulted in waves of Jewish immigration into western Europe as well as to the Americas. And western European Jews, on the whole, welcomed east European Jews no more enthusiastically than their gentile compatriots did. For one thing, many western Jews identified more closely with the gentiles among whom they lived than with the Jews who arrived from the shtetls and towns of eastern Europe. What is more, they were afraid that these "backward" and "primitive" immigrants would provoke anti-Semitic reactions against themselves. Although many west European Jews were socialists or communists, many others were conservative and reactionary. There is every reason to think that many Jewish Germans would have gone along with, or actively supported, National Socialism like other Germans. Because of the Nazis' virulent anti-Semitism and racialism they didn't have that option.

I must confess that I am writing you all this in part to figure out why my sense of Jewish identity is so different from that of most American Jews. And what I have come to is that the basic difference is that most Jews came to America from eastern Europe and have a different, more culturally and ritually focused heritage than I have. Assimilation was less possible in eastern Europe and during the few moments in history when it could happen, it required a greater denial of Jewish identity.

I grew up as a Jew, but without Jewish customs, holidays, celebrations. What gave us identity and held us together was a way of looking at our surroundings that was a mix of outsider feelings (as Jews) blended into an insider national and local identification (as Austrians and Viennese), that particular sense of humor we call "Jewish humor," and our inevitable encounters with anti-Semitism. This may seem a pale Jewishness to people who feel they are part of Jewish culture, but it would be false for me to pretend to the latter experience. I feel European more than Jewish and although I would not want to deny my Jewishness, I also don't want to build it up into something it isn't.

I don't think it's that different from the way many of my friends feel who grew up Catholic, but no longer participate in Catholic rituals. They continue to consider themselves Catholic (or "ex-Catholic") and have a special sense of insiderness toward others who share the same background. I enjoy being among Jews the way "ex-Catholics" like being among "ex-Catholics," or Blacks among Blacks. There is an identification in it that has nothing to do with religion and ritual. But I resent being considered somehow less Jewish, meaning less self-identified as Jewish, than more religious Jews. Jewishness is a history as well as a set of observances and I am part of that history.

The quest for "roots" among feminists has driven many Jewish feminists to identify more strongly with Jewish rituals and culture than they did as recently as ten years ago. Yet most Jewish feminists are politically progressive and anti-imperialist, at least as regards U.S. foreign policy. That has put many of them in a difficult position vis-à-vis Israel, which joins the United States in all its most outrageous attacks on freedom (Vietnam, Chile, Grenada, Cuba, Nicaragua, South Africa, and so on) and perpetrates its own outrages against the former inhabitants of Israel, the Palestinians. The few Palestinian feminists in the United States—and there are a number—have a dreadful time getting heard, and never are heard without a "balancing" Zionist voice, whereas of course pro-Zionist Jews are listened to without even the thought that one should also be hearing from Palestinians. And that brings up the unfortunate equation of "Jewish" with "Zionist" or "pro-Israel," which means that any non-Jew who speaks out against Israeli policies is accused of being anti-Semitic and any Jew who does it, of being self-hating. I identify myself as a Jewish anti-Zionist. Speak of outsider! Of course, as usual, I'm not alone. By the way, is that how you identify yourself?

Ruth being arrested at Otis/Camp Edwards during a protest against sending U.S. National Guard troops to Honduras, 1985.

There are quite a number of us, but it is, shall we say, a minority position and makes us outsiders among Jewish feminists, most of whom support the state of Israel even when they oppose many of its policies. I believe that the state of Israel is tainted at its root and should never have been founded, because it is founded on the expropriation of the native population of that land. Nothing anyone says justifies the fact that I can go to Jaffa and build myself a house there whereas the family on whose land I build it cannot even visit. It's as simple as that. That and the fact that Israel is a religious state that differentiates among people on the basis of religion and racial origins. I realize that any future accommodation must take account of the present reality, including the existence of the Zionist state, but I begin from the recognition that that existence is based on an act of international piracy, like the existence of the white minority government of South Africa.

Speaking of South Africa and being an outsider, I want to tell you about a friend of mine, who is a white woman recently arrived from South Africa. Talking with her, I realize that her outsiderness is more total and complex than any we have thought about so far. She is third generation South African, so more African than you or I are American. She is an outsider in her country and family because of her anti-Apartheid politics. She is not Black, therefore an outsider in the Black struggle. She cannot travel in most of Africa because most countries won't let her in because she is a white South African. (Interestingly, she can travel in Zimbabwe and people treat her well there.) She cannot meet with political allies from abroad because they won't come to South Africa. When she travels outside Africa, especially in Britain and the United States, she keeps running into people who tell her that they realize that what they read about South Africa is propaganda, that they are sure her government is doing the best it can about a very difficult situation. So, as she says, she is left with the choice of getting into a political fight with total strangers or ending such conversations and scurrying off, which is what she usually does. She is an outsider to all but a small group of comrades who are in the same boat as she, since the main opposition movement in South Africa is Black.

Beyond all that, having read Lessing and Gordimer, I have often wondered how it must feel to be white and love Africa as one's home, love its landscape the way you love your New Mexican mountains or I love the Danube or Alt Aussee or the beach here in Woods Hole. (I just notice that I am not at all acknowledging the European colonization of this continent. We are outsiders here much as my friend is in Africa, but few people rub our noses in that.) To love the place where one knows damn well one shouldn't be, yet there is no other place where one belongs because that's where one's ancestors went and where one grew up—which is what we usually mean by "home"—what can be more outside/inside than that? And there are no individual solutions, and the collective solutions are very far off, with lots of anguish between here and there. Being a woman on top of it all in the very sexist white *and* Black cultures of South Africa . . . the complexity and intensity of that kind of outsiderness must be enormous.

To get back to being Jewish, I want to leave my personal experience and politics and think a bit about what happened in Nazi Germany. It brings up a distinction I fumbled toward at the very beginning of our correspondence between outsider and outcast. However much I might have wanted to debase myself and become an outsider to myself, I could not have become an insider in Nazi Austria because I have four Jewish grandparents, period. The Black person in South Africa has black skin and that's it. There is nothing we could, or can, do that would make us anything but outsiders, and that's very different from the way you and I have been using the term. That's why we need a third term, outcast. The more I think of it, the more "outsider," as I have experienced and defined it, implies a measure of taking power, control, and a position in the world—a "here I am and from here I will act." That's true even of my South African friend, who is an outsider in so many dimensions, but can use her outsider status as a way to define herself and a base from which to act politically.

But then there's the outcast. A woman I used to know well, Ilona Karmel, many years ago wrote a book called *An Estate of Memory,* * a novel that Feminist Press has recently reprinted. It was

* *An Estate of Memory* by Ilona Karmel. New York: Feminist Press, 1986.

barely noticed the first time around and I'm holding my breath this time. I think the reason it does not get the attention it merits, and why I cannot get past the first chapter or so (and it's a long book), is that it is about a group of women in Auschwitz and the setting and everything that happens in the book are so overwhelming that I cannot transcend them and most readers probably have the same problem. It is unbelievably awful. But I knew her well while she was writing it and she called it a funny book, meaning that it was full of humorous incidents. What she wanted to show was that people try to live the best lives they can and make the warmest relationships they can, no matter how dreadful the circumstances. So, the book is about an insider space a group of women tried to construct even in hell. I cannot get beyond the hell; she wants to use that hell as a backdrop like any other. In the midst of hunger, disease, starvation, brutal guards, death, these are the lives people made for themselves. (My friend Dolita tells me that this is also how Genovese describes Black people's efforts to make meaningful lives together under slavery.*)

The same theme is echoed in *Mothers in the Fatherland*,** a book by Claudia Koonz, a feminist historian writing about Nazi women and the women who resisted Nazism. A thesis of her book and one of the things she explores in it is the fact that the Nazis' violent misogyny gave the Nazi women's organizations and their leaders an essentially free hand. The men didn't pay any attention to them as long as they took care of the homes, children, and husbands. In that space Nazi women created a ghastly women's world of which they were proud. And this is how she writes about the opposition, and it's interesting from our perspective:

> Where Nazi power reigned, men and women remained separated by function, personality, and responsibilities. Beyond the limits of Hitler's authority, however, in small islands of opposition, women and men formed integrated communities, unified by trust

* *Roll, Jordan, Roll* by Eugene D. Genovese. New York: Vintage Books, 1976.
** *Mothers in the Fatherland* by Claudia Koonz. New York: St. Martin's Press, 1987.

and integrity. After the first wave of isolated and failed protests in 1933, resisters prepared for a long fight. Jews, devastated at their friends' betrayal, created new sources of support that likewise bound together men and women, young and old, rich and poor. To "resist" meant first of all to survive emotionally. It required the inner strength to cut oneself entirely loose from external systems of rewards and punishments and fashion a balance between conformity and opposition . . . Ruth Andreas-Friedrich and her husband, both members of the resistance, wrote: "The time of the lone wolf had passed . . . Strength no longer depended upon those who appeared powerful. We had to build our own troops . . . what one person needs the other will supply. Everything depends on our ability to divide up the roles intelligently."

It seems to me that this clarifies the distinction between outcast and outsider. Under the Nazis, Jews became out*casts* and that was agony, disempowerment. But then, some were able (and I'm sure for external as well as internal reasons) to detach themselves and become conscious out*siders* which gave them the possibility and strength to construct insider enclaves built on mutual need, support, trust.

And talking about the Nazi women, Koonz writes:

Loyal Nazis fashioned an image for themselves, a fake domestic realm where they felt virtuous. Nazi women facilitated that mirage by doing what women have done in other societies—they made the world a more pleasant place in which to live for the members of their community. And they simultaneously made life first unbearable and later impossible for "racially un-worthy" citizens. As fanatical Nazis or lukewarm tag-alongs, they resolutely turned their heads away from assaults against socialists, Jews, religious dissenters, the handicapped, and "degenerates." They gazed instead at their own cradles, children, and "Aryan" families.

> Mothers and wives ... made a vital contribution to
> Nazi power by preserving the illusion of love in an
> environment of hatred, just as men sustained the image
> of order in the utter disarray of conflicting bureau-
> cratic and military priorities and commands.

Koonz does a wonderful job of showing how Nazi women created outsiders and outcasts, and right beside them the inside space in which they could listen to Mozart and Beethoven while the chimneys belched human smoke.

Later, towards the end of the book, when writing about Jewish women, she analyzes the ways they tried to develop insider spaces in their ghastly outsider existences that made it possible for a few of them to survive. And it's very much like Ilona Karmel's novel. They are writing about the same thing, except that Koonz doesn't overwhelm me with the agonizing day-by-day realities of the women's existence, so that I can think about them and listen better.

Koonz writes that of the three hundred thousand Jewish Germans who were deported, only five thousand survived (so, about one in sixty) whereas of the approximately twenty thousand who went underground, about two-thirds survived, so twelve or thirteen thousand. I had always assumed that going underground was sure death. She shows that if you somehow managed to do that, you had a much better chance of surviving. And although she doesn't use that language, what she is in fact saying is that to go underground meant to decide to cut yourself off from past, family, identity—become an outsider even to yourself in order to build a new quasi-inside (with the help of others, if possible, but not necessarily) in hopes of surviving and eventually, when it's over, finding your way back to your former self and your friends and family.

Those who didn't have the resources, and weren't situated so as to be able to do that, kept trying to find ways in which they could stay in some sort of inside within the outside—find loopholes in their outcast status: men claiming special rights because they were veterans, women because of family obligations, or whatever. Initially such "special" circumstances granted them tiny specks of space inside, until they were trapped beyond escaping and

191

deported. And then, in the camps with all their ghastliness, when families were deliberately separated, women (better than men, she says) tried to forge new ties, make new inside spaces where they could gain an emotional hold and make a life together. Men needed their "feminine" qualities, their abilities to enter into mutually supportive relationships to have a chance to get out alive. To learn "to share, trust, and comfort one another, admit their fears, and to hope together. But most men had to learn behaviors women already knew. . ." Koonz quotes from the diary of a Jewish woman inmate in Ravensbruck: "One thing here upsets me terribly, and that is to see that the men are far weaker and far less able to stand up to hardship than the women—physically and often morally as well. Unable to control themselves, they display such a lack of moral fiber that one cannot but be sorry for them . . . To be sure, however, their behavior here is merely a natural continuation of their past." The skills women had learned to create an "inside" in which to support and love each other, she says, were crucial for survival.

I guess I have traveled a long way from where I started this letter, but it's all part of what I think goes into being insider and outsider in relation to being Jewish.

Enough for today!

Much love,

Ruth

Letter Eighteen

Hartford, Connecticut
October 10, 1987

Dearest Ruth:

About the time I was writing to you about the Jewish part of my identity, you were writing to me about the same issue. Of course your letter made me realize I left some questions unanswered, so I'll try to answer them here—before going on to anything else.

You identify yourself as a Jewish anti-Zionist. I wouldn't reject that identification for myself, but neither do I feel it says most importantly what I am, in an ethnic or any other sense. Whereas you grew up with a consciousness of being Jewish, and went on to suffer what was surely the most wrenching experience of your life because you were Jewish, as a child I really had no racial or cultural family identity. My only early contact with a sense of being Jewish was through my paternal grandmother, but even in her home there was no ritual in which I participated.

As I said in my last letter, in spite of never having received a Jewish upbringing, either culturally or religiously, I nevertheless somehow always thought of myself as "coming from a Jewish family." I knew the history of Nazi persecution, my father's father had come over from Germany, and even as a small child I felt a blind indignant rage when the holocaust was mentioned. What's more, as I've said, I passed this vague sense of Jewishness on to my children. But, if I had never held Jewish religious beliefs, never participated in any Jewish ritual such as lighting the sabbath candles, and never had a connection of any kind with the culture —language, music, stories—what about me was Jewish? When asked, rather than say "I am Jewish," I would say "I come from a Jewish family," meaning my family in my grandparents' generation and before.

This kind of identity problem, by the way, has been much more present in my particular life with regard to my "Latinness" than with regard to whether or not I claimed a Jewish heritage. I lived for twenty-three years in Latin America, all of my children were raised there, I even came (at a certain point) to write some of my books in Spanish. As far as I know my family roots have nothing to do with any Latin culture, and yet there have been times in my life when I have found it difficult to separate the Latin and "Anglo" pieces of my identity.

To get back to your question, though, I would still say: I am a person of Jewish heritage; I will not deny a part of my history that has been so brutalized and discriminated against. I am a person of Jewish heritage who has no real roots in Jewish cultural practice nor in Judaism as a religion. Like you, I am anti-Zionist, and for the same reasons. When I contemplate the way a position on Israel has split Jewish feminists and other Jews in this country, I remind myself that in Israel too there are anti-Zionists. And I remind myself of Lisa Kokin's batique when emotions flare and people (on both sides) lose sight of fundamental issues of human rights and mediation.

What I really wanted to write about today is invasion. I keep going back to the letter in which you speak about insider/outsider-ness with regard to the medical invasion of a woman's womb—in procedures like the ultrasound scan, amniocentesis and so-called fetal therapy. (Maybe this is on my mind because I have just become a grandmother! My son Gregory and my daughter-in-law Laura have just had their first child, in Paris; her name is Lia Margarita, and she was born October 7th.) But rather than dwell on the insider/outsider issues concerning our reproductive rights (perhaps because you have spoken so eloquently about them, and I find myself agreeing with all you have said), it's got me to thinking more about the dynamic in terms of all kinds of invasion.

Assuming wholeness as a basic and non-negotiable require-
ment for being inside (inside your basic human right to exist as a
complete and functioning entity), we can move to consider invasion
of whatever kind as being pulled out of oneself, a particular assault
which in some fundamental way threatens not only the wholeness of
the moment but future wholeness as well.

A nation invaded becomes a nation whose insider/outsider
balance has been disturbed. It is then not simply the same nation it
was before except that it has been invaded. Its internal as well as
external boundaries are changed. It must engage in continuous
struggle to regain its integrity. This struggle becomes a part of its
identity. Now it's a nation whose very nature (identity) has been
altered; an essential part of its insiderness has been disfigured,
pulled outside of itself.

Cuba and Nicaragua are excellent examples of this.

Cuba's close to three decades of revolution have from the
beginning been conditioned, among other things, by U.S. attempts
to bring the revolution down. That hostility has ranged from
repeated outright military invasion to literally thousands of
examples of economic assault, biological warfare, assassination
attempts on Cuban leaders, a barrage of ideological attacks, low
intensity warfare; you name it.

Revolutionary Cuba would have been another nation, with different contours, a different texture, a richer peace, more success in
its achievements, were it not for the inordinate energies required
simply to defend its right to exist.

When the Cubans decided for humanitarian reasons in 1978 to
open the country up to visits from the exiles who had left, tens of
thousands returned for short stays. But they didn't come alone. They
came bearing suitcases full of "free world" consumer products
(unavailable on the island primarily because of the U.S.-imposed
blockade). With this cargo they put into motion an on-going and
insidious dynamic: the exiles would justify having left by flaunting
the spoils of "freedom"; the Cubans who had stayed would be torn
by the lure of unobtainable goods. This dynamic, of course, has
grossly complicated Cuba's insider/outsider issues with regard to its
exile community.

In another arena, those who have shared Cuba's struggle have no trouble understanding Fidel Castro's 1962 Words to the Intellectuals: " . . . Within the Revolution, everything; outside the Revolution, nothing . . . because the Revolution also has its rights, and the first right of the Revolution is to be, to exist." Essential words in the mouth of a tiny and besieged nation, forced to draw on every resource beginning with its culture, in order to survive. Even much of the left intelligentsia in other countries, perhaps because for it much of the insider/outsider struggle remains an intellectual exercise, immediately interpreted those words as an infringement of artistic freedom. Cuban intellectuals felt that they and their work were being taken seriously—for the first time in their history.

The Sandinista revolution in Nicaragua is being forced to resist a similar distorting siege. Its defensive requirements have also changed its present and future face. Its insider/outsider balance has consequently been affected.

These events seem relevant in great and small contexts, to individuals as well as to nations.

A prisoner who has been tortured irrevocably loses a part of him- or herself; from that moment on everything the tortured person does or is includes that fact within itself. For a woman who has been raped, for a child who has survived incest or other abuse, the phenomenon is similar. Something is changed, something is lost, something which it may take a lifetime to regain. Often, when the invasion (of body, of psyche, of spirit) takes place early enough, even coming to recognize that there is a wholeness missing may be a monumental task. Sometimes, I suppose, an impossible one.

We have both spoken of the strength—the insiderness— attainable within these struggles themselves. But the invasion has been perpetrated. If the subsequent struggle brings a nation or an individual inside, it has been the reward for extraordinary resistance. The resultant insiderness includes within itself the dynamic of that struggle.

The ability to bond in certain ways constitutes a wholeness subject as well to invasion. When you talk about the male medical club making it seem unsafe for a woman to retain the mystery (to them) of her own womb, I think you are talking about this invasion in a very profound way. It seems an even further extension of the practice of forcing caesarean sections on absurd numbers of women who do not need them simply because it assures more money and a more predictable schedule of births for the profession; that initial contact between mother and newborn child is lost, not to mention the invasion of both bodies: one by being cut open, the other by being denied its natural journey out of the womb.

Perhaps this is a clue as to why boundaries and the invasion of boundaries is such a vulnerable area in relationships of all kinds. For multiple reasons we often cannot see or feel the boundary lines essential to others, even (or especially!) those closest to us. Not seeing or feeling them, we may invade them, may enter a space that is unwilling or unable to accept our presence. This happens often in the close, intense, relationship between lovers. The insider/outsider balance is then disturbed—perhaps without a consciousness on either person's part, perhaps only with a consciousness on the invaded person's part, that this has happened.

I have always believed that what happens between individuals is a microcosm of what happens between nations; inversely, what happens between nations is a macro version of what goes on between the two people in a couple or between parents and children, teacher and taught, doctor and client. When power is not equally shared, when both parties don't initiate and sustain all contact from an absolute bedrock of mutual respect, we're in trouble.

One of the reasons Judith McDaniel and I do such a powerful reading from her book on sanctuary and my book on incest* is that we link the personal and political spheres along invasion's insider/outsider line. People—mostly women, I think—who have worked in solidarity with Central America but ignored their own (probably invaded) lives come to see personal invasion in political terms. People—again mostly women—who have explored their own maps and memories but felt they couldn't get involved in politics, also make the connections. I think women are more open to making these connections because for historical reasons we have a fiercer need to reclaim our inside space.

Way back in our first letters on this subject I remember we noticed that one is always somehow simultaneously inside and outside, insider and outsider. Assuming that this is so, would it

* *Sanctuary, A Journey* and *This is About Incest* by Judith McDaniel and Margaret Randall, respectively. Ithaca, NY: Firebrand Books, 1987.

Margaret reading poetry in New York City, 1984. (Photo: Judy Janda)

make sense, then, to speak of a balance between the two conditions, and of this balance itself as strengthening as well our insiderness—conversely, an imbalance pulling us more outside?

Much love,

Margaret

Letter Nineteen

Woods Hole, Massachusetts
October 12th, 1987

Dearest Margaret:

I want to write briefly about whether women as a group are outsiders, irrespective of our position in the world. I know that many feminists—radical feminists, cultural feminists, call them what you will—believe that, but I cannot. Yes, women as a gender are outside the male power structure. But so are women and men as Blacks, as other minorities, and as other than ruling class. So, I can't say "women as gender" or "men as gender" because when class and race get in there, these genders are very heterogeneous. Are Margaret Thatcher or Sandra Day O'Connor not part of women as gender? Are they outsiders in the same sense that poor women are outsiders because of their common gender? I don't see that. Thatcher and O'Connor may indeed be outsiders because of their gender compared to Reagan or Rehnquist, but they are a hell of a lot more insiders than most men. So, I don't really find the concept of "women as gender" very useful and usually don't use it.

If gender were the only operative category, women would be by definition outsiders, maybe outcasts. Since it is not, we may be gender-outcasts, but we can be insiders by virtue of our race and class positions, especially if we are willing to behave the way the men in power say women should behave. So, in that sense, women are not as definitive outcasts in this society as Jews were in Nazi Germany. Because there was nothing a Jew could do that would make him or her anything but an outcast. Even a cooperating Jew, a member of the Judenrat, who helped select the Jews who were shipped off to the gas chambers, did not thereby become an insider. He may have survived (and I believe they all were "he"), but as an outcast. Do you agree with the way I am formulating this?

Ruth and family at anti-war demonstration, Boston, 1970

I find the intersection of race, class, and gender so powerful that I cannot accept that gender alone confers insider status on men (incarcerated men? junkies? mine workers in South Africa?) and outsider status on women. In fact, the very notion of "all women" (or "all men") troubles me. Women can be very different from one another, as can men, and there are many physical and psychological similarities between women and men, as groups. Nothing I know of holds for all women or all men. So, I cannot accept the idea of gender per se determining insider or outsider status and don't think it is theoretically or politically useful to think in those terms.

Much love,

Ruth

Letter Twenty

Hartford, Connecticut
October 18th, 1987

Dearest Ruth:

When we say that for us the most important thing about insider/outsider is the tension created between the poles, a great many of my intuitive feelings fall into place. The tension is like a motor that propels us through our lives. And the power switch is always "ON."

I see the tension between the ways in which we are defined and define ourselves simultaneously as insider and outsider. And I agree, we are both, always. That's why I am interested in being able to demystify in both directions at once; so that our sense of self as well as our movement through sociopolitical space may ride on the cutting edge of that insider/outsider tension. It's like three-dimensional chess, on an almost infinite number of superimposed levels. In my life, a bottom-line indicator is my womanhood.

And this is where we may or may not have a difference of opinion. (I say we may or may not, because some of your formulations lead me to believe we have a semantic, rather than an ideological problem.)

Gender, unlike class, is (almost always) definitive. Like race, it is virtually immutable, and offers fewer opportunities for passing. For me, it is a given which has also become a home. For this and other reasons I question the statement in your first letter: "Take being a woman: outsider to the male power structure. But in a sense, so are most men."

Of course a few (white) men make up the real power structure in this country, and in that sense other men—non-white, less economically secure, from newer family traditions, not as well educated within the establishment—are outside. But when I consider women as outside the male power structure I am not thinking of individual women; it is precisely here that I am talking about women as gender.

If gender were the only criterion, all men would have access to the power structure and no women would. The fact that all men don't have this access tells us that gender is not the only determinant. There is class, there is race, and there are also characteristics like ablebodyness, sexual preference, culture, education, family, tradition.

But when race, class, and other factors are the same and the only difference between two people is that one is a man and the other is a woman, that's where gender comes into play. For example, you mention prisoners. I read an article recently that pointed out that in the New Mexico prisons there are men serving months for rape and women serving years for passing a bad check; men serving ten years for first degree murder and women serving life sentences for having killed their husbands in proven self-defense. There, clearly, gender is an issue. (In this same article we can see that a Black woman received a stiffer sentence than a white woman for no other apparent reason than her blackness. And this is clearly true of men who have been lynched throughout our history for simply looking at white women—or for not doing anything. Of course I am not denying the racial issue, only saying there is a gender issue.)

And this is precisely why I'm always telling my students (and everyone else): if you only look at gender you will be wrong. If you only look at class you will be wrong. If you only look at race you will be wrong. You will only be right—that is, on the road towards some partial answers—if you look at the places where class, race, gender, and some of the other criteria come together.

Are we searching for some point along the Dutch Cleanser progression? Are we simply training our eyes so they may focus on a more and more distant place along a linear continuum? Or is it an imaginary dot along the Möbius strip, a juncture the precise nature of which we cannot yet predict?

You single out Margaret Thatcher and Sandra Day O'Connor as women who in many important ways share in the power structure more than most men. I agree. But I see them sharing in the power structure *because* of their class, or the ways in which they have otherwise been allowed into the system, and *in spite of* their gender. So I would say that class-wise and/or in other ways they are indeed insiders, but *as women* they are still outside.

We can make the same distinctions when talking about race. Take Jesse Jackson. He is an insider by virtue of his gender, an insider by virtue of his political experience and charisma, but he is outside in his blackness and also in terms of his progressive politics. Because of his male insiderness he is able to run for the nomination for president within one of the two establishment political parties. No woman has yet been able to do that. Because of his racial and political outsiderness he probably cannot be nominated, much less elected, president in the United States at this point in time.

All I'm really saying here is that I find it useful to speak of class, race, gender, and other categorical definitions. But in our society these must come together in a single human being for him or her to be inside in a way that makes a concrete difference.

Why do I see my womanhood—more than my class or race—as essential to who I am? Perhaps because I am privileged by both class and race. And then there is another, gut, answer to that: I love being a woman. I do not love my bourgeois class origin. I have made peace with it, which is not the same. I have left behind the unconscious arrogance of class that marked my childhood, and the useless guilt about it that laced my young adulthood. I have come to understand how we can learn to use class rather than allow it to use us, how class privilege can be used for what it offers in resources of all kinds, and what class betrayal might mean within a particular life.

I do not love being white. In fact, I have often resented it, bemoaned it, seen it as an impediment to whatever integration I might have been seeking at a particular time and place. Issues of race, like those of class, can be pushed into extremist shapes. It is also easy to be a liberal and ignore them. We struggle for a balance we can live with.

With my womanness, though, I have struggled through my share of social conditioning to a place where mind and gut, body and soul, have come into a pretty clear focus. And that focus is due in great part to the fact that I have not struggled alone. Unlike the Georgia O'Keeffes and Alice Hamiltons who made my own way easier, the struggle has given me community and this community has become a part of my identity.

This, then, is one of the essential things I want to say about my condition as insider/outsider: being a woman both defines an inside identity within my conception of self and defines me as outside in the misogynist social construct.

Much, much love,

Margaret

Letter Twenty-One

Woods Hole, Massachusetts
October 22, 1987

Dearest Margaret:

As this phase of our correspondence winds up, I want to clarify what appears to be a genuine difference between the ways we see gender impact on our insider/outsider constellations. But first I need to clear up a misunderstanding that I don't think reflects a real difference between us.

Early in your last letter you cite prison statistics to the effect that in New Mexico men are serving sentences of months for rape while women serve years for passing bad checks and so on, and use this to argue that women are disadvantaged "as a gender." You also observe that race is important, and I know that you believe class is as well. But, for this very reason, breaking sentences down only by gender misrepresents the way the so-called criminal justice system operates. When it comes to people in the American prisons, it is not enough to look at whether they are women or men. The more revealing questions are: what women, which men? Surely in New Mexico, as elsewhere in this country, Black or Chicano men do not get only months for raping a *white* woman (unless she happens to be a prostitute, which may override her skin color). After all, we live in a country where race—and of course class—determine not just the severity of the sentence, but who gets accused, arrested, tried, convicted, or sentenced at all. Gender enters in, but all these combine to determine who ends up in prison and for how long.

On our visit to Cuba, our hosts took us to the big prison outside Havana. (I forget its name.) Debbie, who had been working with women incarcerated at the Massachusetts women's prison in Framingham, kept looking to see whether the range of skin colors was comparable to what we were seeing on the street. It was. But obviously it's not that way here.

As I say, I don't think this is a point of disagreement between us. I would say that you were getting a superficial, hence biased, report and I expect you'd agree. Where we differ is on your final statement and I'll quote it because it is so straight-forward and strong: "being a woman both defines an inside identity within my conception of self and defines me as outside in the misogynist social construct."

For me, too, being a woman defines my insiderness—personally (in my family and with my friends), professionally (in women's studies), and politically (in the women's liberation and women's health movements). But I see my outsiderness as varied and multi-faceted and do not privilege my gender over the other contours of my outsider landscape: the fact that I am old, that I am both Jewish and anti-Zionist, a professional woman, a dissident scientist, all the things we have been writing about and no doubt more. All these define who I am by delineating what I am not and I value the varied range of my outsiderness.

I am content to have this conversation end on a difference between us and hope you are as well. I am sure our feelings reflect our different experiences, those we have written about and others. Best of all, it means we have to keep talking.

Much, much love,

Ruth

About the Authors

Ruth Hubbard was born in 1924 in Vienna, Austria. She and her parents left Austria shortly after the Nazi takeover in 1938, and came to the United States as refugees. She received her A.B. in Biochemical Sciences and her Ph.D. in Biology from Radcliffe College. She is a Professor of Biology at Harvard University. She has edited and contributed to books on feminist analyses of science and written about women's biology and health for professional journals and other periodicals.

Margaret Randall was born in 1936 in New York City. She is a writer, photographer and teacher who lived for half her life in Latin America and recently returned to the United States. She has published over 50 books of poetry, prose, oral history, and photography. Some of her most recent titles are: *Albuquerque: Coming Home to the USA, This is About Incest,* and *Memory Says Yes.* Since her return to the United States, the Immigration and Naturalization Service has been trying to deport her, claiming her writing is too critical of the U.S. government's policy in Latin America. In the spring of 1989, she will be the Hubert H. Humphrey Visiting Professor of International Affairs at Macalester College in Saint Paul, Minnesota.

Books from Cleis Press

AIDS: The Women edited by Ines Rieder and Patricia Ruppelt. ISBN: 0-939416-20-4 24.95 cloth; ISBN: 0-939416-21-2 9.95 paper.

The Shape of Red: Insider/Outsider Reflections by Ruth Hubbard and Margaret Randall. ISBN: 0-939416-19-0, 24.95 cloth; ISBN: 0-939416-18-2 9.95 paper

You Can't Drown the Fire: Latin American Women Writing in Exile edited by Alicia Partnoy. ISBN: 0-939416-16-6 24.95 cloth; ISBN: 0-939416-17-4 9.95 paper.

Unholy Alliances: New Women's Fiction edited by Louise Rafkin. ISBN: 0-939416-14-X 21.95 cloth; ISBN: 0-939416-15-8 9.95 paper.

Sex Work: Writings by Women in the Sex Industry edited by Frédérique Delacoste and Priscilla Alexander. ISBN: 0-939416-10-7 24.95 cloth; ISBN: 0-939416-11-5 10.95 paper.

Different Daughters: A Book by Mothers of Lesbians edited by Louise Rafkin. ISBN: 0-939416-12-3 21.95 cloth; ISBN: 0-939416-13-1 8.95 paper.

The Little School: Tales of Disappearance & Survival in Argentina by Alicia Partnoy. ISBN: 0-939416-08-5 21.95 cloth; ISBN: 0-939416- 07-7 8.95 paper.

With the Power of Each Breath: A Disabled Women's Anthology edited by Susan Browne, Debra Connors & Nanci Stern. ISBN: 0-939416-09-3 24.95 cloth; ISBN: 0-939416-06-9 9.95 paper.

Voices in the Night: Women Speaking About Incest edited by Toni A.H. McNaron & Yarrow Morgan. ISBN: 0-939416-02-6 9.95 paper.

Long Way Home: The Odyssey of a Lesbian Mother & Her Children by Jeanne Jullion. ISBN: 0-939416-05-0 8.95 paper.

The Absence of the Dead Is Their Way of Appearing by Mary Winfrey Trautmann. ISBN: 0-939416-04-2 8.95 paper.

Woman-Centered Pregnancy & Birth by the Federation of Feminist Women's Health Centers. ISBN: 0-939416-03-4 11.95 paper.

Fight Back! Feminist Resistance to Male Violence edited by Frédérique Delacoste & Felice Newman. ISBN: 0-939416-01-8 13.95 paper.

On Women Artists: Poems 1975-1980 by Alexandra Grilikhes. ISBN: 0-939416-00-X 4.95 paper.

Cleis Press is a nine-year-old women's publishing company committed to publishing progressive books by women. Order from the office nearest you: Cleis East, PO Box 8933, Pittsburgh PA 15221 or Cleis West, PO Box 14684, San Francisco CA 94114. Individual orders must be prepaid, including shipping (1.50 for the first book; .75 for each additional book). PA and CA residents add sales tax. MasterCard and Visa orders welcome—include account number, exp. date, and signature.